D1710948

Greenhouse
GARDENING

The Ultimate Step-by-Step Gardener's Manual for Beginners to Grow Healthy Vegetables, Herbs, and Fruits All-Year-Round and learn How to Make A Good Profit from your Greenhouse.

Tyler Water

© Copyright Tyler Water 2021 All rights reserved.

The content contained within this book may not be reproduced, duplicated or transmitted without direct written permission from the author or the publisher.

Under no circumstances will any blame or legal responsibility be held against the publisher, or author, for any damages, reparation, or monetary loss due to the information contained within this book. Either directly or indirectly.

Legal Notice:

This book is copyright protected. This book is only for personal use. You cannot amend, distribute, sell, use, quote or paraphrase any part, or the content within this book, without the consent of the author or publisher.

Disclaimer Notice:

Please note the information contained within this document is for educational and entertainment purposes only. All effort has been executed to present accurate, up to date, and reliable, complete information. No warranties of any kind are declared or implied. Readers acknowledge that the author is not engaging in the rendering of legal, financial, medical or professional advice. The content within this book has been derived from various sources. Please consult a licensed professional before attempting any techniques outlined in this book.

By reading this document, the reader agrees that under no circumstances is the author responsible for any losses, direct or indirect, which are incurred as a result of the use of information contained within this document, including, but not limited to, — errors, omissions, or inaccuracies.

Table of Contents

INTRODUCTION

G ardening in the comfort of your own home has never been easier. Before you start, here are a few things to keep in mind.

While there is no right or wrong ways to garden, sometimes you need to see things from the other side of the fence. Keeping a record of what works for you will help you do it more efficiently.

Some tips and tricks for getting started:

- Choose a place that is sunny all day. When deciding on a location, consider whether you will have access to water or electricity. When planning a garden, make sure the structure does not block nearby windows from receiving direct sunlight during the day. If your garden is located near a window, consider how much sun you do get during the day. If it is not enough, consider moving your garden location to one that has more sun exposure.

- Choose a place that is sunny all day. When deciding on a location, consider whether you will have access to water or electricity. When planning a garden, make sure the structure does not block nearby windows from receiving direct sunlight during the day. If your garden is located near a window, consider how much sun you do get during the day. If it is not enough, consider moving your garden location to one that has more sun exposure. - Plant deep-rooted plants so they can grow vertically and reach their full potential instead of sprawling over the entire area. Deep-rooted plants include tulip trees, flowering shrubs and hardy perennials that live up to five years before needing replacement. In addition, these plants form roots at soil level instead of at ground level where they can become damaged by pests and diseases.

- Plant deep-rooted plants so they can grow vertically and reach their full potential instead of sprawling over the entire area. Deep-rooted plants include tulip trees, flowering shrubs and hardy perennials that live up to five years before needing replacement.

To many gardeners, the word "gardening" refers to planting annuals and potted plants in containers. Gardening can be as exciting as you make it, and there are many ways to do it right.

So, why would you garden? In today's world of backyard home construction, and especially climate change, greenhouse gardening has become a common way to extend the growing season so that you can continue to enjoy flowers all year round. You can also grow plants that are hard to cultivate in other weather conditions, including orchids and tropical plants.

But you don't have to start from scratch to grow your own food or produce beautiful flowers in your backyard. The Greenhouse Gardening book will show you how to start enjoying all the benefits of growing your own produce even if you don't have a greenhouse. We'll show you how growing vegetables can save money, space and energy, and how colorful flowers can improve the appearance of your backyard while adding beauty to your yard at the same time.

CHAPTER 1

How a Greenhouse Benefits You

Would you believe me when I said that greenhouses don't have to be a huge expense and drain on your budget? While it does seem that gardening is an expensive hobby on the best of days, the greenhouse has some benefits that far outweigh open-air gardens.

With the greenhouse, you limit the number of pests and diseases that affect your plants. This, in turn, saves them in the long run and saves you money since you don't spend as much replacing plants and replanting or treating diseased areas.

Alternatively, the one-time expense a greenhouse might incur for you when it is built will even out since it will save you a pretty penny on your grocery bill.

The greenhouse is quickly becoming a forerunner for maintaining food in areas where food scarcity is a real problem, or where the expense of food has drastically increased. Greenhouses offer families the option to grow their own fruits and vegetables at almost no cost to them. When you think about your grocery bill, I am positive that a large chunk is devoted to those expensive grocery store vegetables.

Greenhouses can be expensive to build — that is if you are not conscious of the types of material that you are using. When deciding to build a greenhouse you should consider the realities of your weather conditions. If you don't live in an area with severe storms and high winds, you'll probably be able to use a cheaper material for your greenhouse.

The Long-Term Plan

It goes without saying that the long-term benefits of the greenhouse are that it saves you money, you know where your food is coming from, and you're able to feed your family chemical-free food.

However, this can be a difficult task to do all on your own. You want the long-term benefits, who doesn't? You don't want to do it alone though. And that makes sense. The world needs the knowledge that you are learning today to be passed onto future generations because it could very well be greenhouse gardening that helps feed families in the future.

Your children need to understand what you are doing and so do other members of your family. That's the only way to truly bring everyone together and build a sustainable future for other generations.

Your greenhouse could be a simple way to feed your family. It could also develop into a business that you one day want your children to take over. There is a reason why family-run farms and greenhouses perform better throughout several generations than other types of family businesses. Gardening brings a family together, and once you start with it there is a distinct pride that is associated with growing your own fruits and vegetables and then enjoying the pickings of your labor.

So, how do you get your family involved with the greenhouse garden? You want them to build a sustainable future and if you teach your family how to garden then at least they will always have one way to provide for themselves nutritionally that doesn't cost them too much financially.

Get your kids involved in gardening right away. They can be three years old or five years old and there are still things that you can do to open their minds to the wonders of growing plants. Your kids will be passionate about things such as greenhouse gardening if they feel involved from a young age. A good way to do this is to give your child the responsibility of one plant to start out with and then increase the plants in their care as they grow and learn. They should be learning everything about the care of that plant, that's how they will get excited about feeding their family.

As your children's and family's skill set begins to grow, then go ahead and increase their responsibility in the greenhouse. We never learn anything if we keep competing at the same level forever, we need to make mistakes and learn new pathways to expand our knowledge and expertise. Try putting your kids in charge of a special flower that will be grown for a parent or loved one for the holiday. Allow them to be in charge of giving the right amount of water to all the plants on a certain bench. Give them new tasks to help you with as they master old ones so that their minds are constantly expanding.

The best advice I can give you to get your family involved is to make it their choice. No one wants to do anything that they feel is being forced upon them. Allow them to see the benefits of greenhouse gardening and when they want to take part in the growing process, encourage them. You will both have a better time when it is their choice to enjoy gardening with you.

CHAPTER 2
Types of Greenhouse

A greenhouse operation's efficiency and productivity are primarily dependent on the growing structure used. Since there are several designs to choose from, it is necessary to become acquainted with the benefits and drawbacks. A short discussion of commercial greenhouses and their structural components is presented below.

Lean-to Greenhouse

A greenhouse is a greenhouse that you create against a wall or another structure's side. It implies that it has its own three walls and shares one wall with another system. This other building is most likely to be your house, but it may also be a shed or another course in your backyard.

This greenhouse style is made up of the same materials as a typical greenhouse. When you look at the right model for you, you are more likely to choose between a greenhouse-lean polycarbonate and a greenhouse-lean glass. In our Greenhouse Beginners Guide, both materials' benefits and drawbacks are explained in depth. For attached greenhouses, all the options for standard greenhouses are also available, such as greenhouse heating and greenhouse insulation. In search of a small addition to your yard. Are you going to go for a significant greenhouse that could double as a sunroom? Your ideal match will be found!

Benefits of a lean greenhouse

You can build your greenhouse directly against your outside wall if you have a smaller backyard but enough room around your home. It's the ideal solution if you don't want to lose too much yard or if your children and spouse have claimed your backyard. You can also use your lean-to greenhouse as a sunroom to hit the greenhouse in your yard without having to gear up in winter clothes!

The key benefits of choosing a lean greenhouse are the following:

- For urban gardening, it is the ideal greenhouse.

- You will get more value for your money when you're just investing in a three-sided greenhouse than when you pick a four-sided greenhouse in the middle of your yard. Since you're going to build it against your steady outside wall, you can make the other three sides a little lighter.

- In your greenhouse, easy access to electricity and Water

- You need less space to build a lean greenhouse, and in smaller versions, you will have a lot of choices.

- They are suitable for growing smaller vegetables and herbs.

- As they are covered by your home and less exposed to the elements, they are very weatherproof.

In general, most people would want a lean greenhouse to save space and probably money, but there are also several more extensive and more costly versions, of course. You can attach your greenhouse through a direct door when you have the budget and space, and it can double as a sitting area to enjoy the sun all year long.

To build your greenhouse, make sure you verify the carrying capacity of the wall you are using. If you want to install a large lean on the greenhouse, work with an architect or contractor. You will also need a building permit in some countries, so get informed before you begin your expansion!

The most significant downside is that there is just light and sun on three sides going in. A typical greenhouse can absorb light from all sides, but it is entirely fixable provided the proper positioning.

Where do you put the greenhouse lean on?

Several factors depend on where the greenhouse should be positioned:

- How much room on either side of your house do you have?

- How broad would you like your greenhouse to be?

Your house's orientation. The most widely used exposure, classically, is Southern. Do not think about it because you don't have enough room on your building's south side. Only try to ensure that your greenhouse gets as much sun as possible during winter. You also know that you will need more cooling during hot summer days when your greenhouse is oriented towards the south. Be prepared to look at possibilities for ventilation!

Where do you have energy and Water on the sides of your house that could be conveniently moved to your greenhouse?

You can go as wide as you want or as small as you want. You can connect the greenhouse with a door to the house or just use the wall to lean on the outside and have a separate entrance. Most other considerations you need to focus on will remain the same as in every other greenhouse when choosing a lean-to-greenhouse model, such as material selection, size, and accessories. Take a look at our guide for greenhouse beginners to help you determine the type of greenhouse that suits you best.

Lean-to Plans for Greenhouse

It is essential to ensure that they not only suit the space you have available but also use materials you can purchase while searching for lean-to greenhouse plans.

From there, it's all about the greenhouse's interior room and how you can reach it. At one end, most have a door: mine has interior windows that open onto our covered patio. It is a shame to waste space if you don't need to access the plants, particularly in a smaller area.

This greenhouse design's full benefit is the cost savings achieved by building your home, garage, or shed next to an existing wall. These savings will make room for some nice-to-have extras, such as automatic window openers, in the budget.

There are many free plans online, but I couldn't find anything in the style or size I needed, so I adapted the existing methods instead.

I began searching online to create a lean-to greenhouse next to a building when I decided to design this greenhouse. My situation is slightly different because it opens to the inside of the covered patio instead of entering the greenhouse from one of the ends. And I decided to establish it at table-height for easy access instead of building it full-height.

This barn greenhouse by Ana White, a freestanding 8-12-foot greenhouse, is the inspiration for the design. The mine is around 3.12-feet. So, to suit my situation, I had to rework the strategy. I swear that it took me longer to think about the plan than it did to build the thing!

I started to use many old wood-framed house windows to have leftovers from a roadside shipment. After some consideration, I realized that the windows, which are all different sizes and environments, would be complicated to frame adequately and obtain the reasonably airtight (and rainproof) room I hoped for. Instead, as you'll see below, I used transparent 12-foot Suntuf polycarbonate exterior panels and three of the old wood windows for the interior window doors.

In the cold months, this greenhouse's primary objective is to grow winter veggies such as salad greens (mesclun mix), spinach, broccoli, Brussels sprouts, and kale propagates spring and fall cuttings. I expect it to be too hot to develop in the summer, but I might test a shade cloth to keep the summer heat down.

While I know it is implausible that you would choose to create a structure precisely as I have done here, if you need ideas for your specific building situation, I will guide you through the process.

And yes, without any support, I created it all by myself. I don't have any special skills, but I just enjoy making things and learning as I go.

There was quite a range of challenges, including the patio itself, which is not level or square, and some of the second-rate wood I bought, which was quite twisted. Still, I managed to make it work, like any ordinary superhero.

Even and Uneven Type Greenhouse

An even-span greenhouse is a greenhouse designed where the roof's pitch is equal in length and angle. It is in comparison with a greenhouse with an uneven duration.

Two basic types of even-span greenhouses are available: American (also referred to as high profile) and Dutch Venlo (also called a low profile). One large roof per structure features American even-span greenhouses. The top has panes that overlap.

There are two small roofs per structure for the Dutch even-span greenhouse. From the eave to the ridge, the panes on the top of a Dutch Venlo even-span greenhouse stretch. There are no overlapping panes, with the Dutch Venlo even-span greenhouse.

Maximum Yield clarifies that also Period Greenhouse.

Because of its relative ease of construction, an even-span greenhouse is one of the most common greenhouse models. The efficient design offers adequate growing space and is typically less expensive than other shapes or types of greenhouses.

Some even-span greenhouses are designed as an attached structure that shares a wall with another network, but it still maintains its symmetrical roof, unlike a lean-to greenhouse. Such a configuration is much more economical to build.

To build a more visually pleasing architectural appearance, even-span greenhouses will also feature curved eaves. There are readily available prefabricated even-span greenhouses for purchase.

Uneven Type Greenhouse

A greenhouse with a slope of one roof more extended than the other is an uneven-span greenhouse. In general, when it is located on hilly terrain or to take advantage of solar angles, this is an adaptation of a standard greenhouse.

The roof is not equal in width or pitch in uneven-span greenhouses, hence the name, and the steeper angle faces the south. The south's side is translucent for energy saving, while the other side facing the north is opaque.

Uneven-span greenhouses are no longer as popular, as most greenhouses are being constructed on flat land today.

Uneven Period Greenhouse clarified by Maximum Yield.

When building a greenhouse, several variables must be taken into account. Until building can begin, various elements must be looked at for greenhouse design and technology selection. Greenhouse types may range from small, stand-alone structures to large, gutter-connected greenhouses according to the necessary functions. There are many styles and systems to choose from, such as greenhouses with uneven spans and greenhouses with even spans. Consequently, they all have their perks and drawbacks.

The benefit of making an uneven greenhouse is that the hillsides perform very well. The longer side of the roof allows for more sunshine to reach the greenhouse without the side walls or rafters obstructing it. The roof's longer side faces the south, which maximizes the sun's heat rays.

Ridge and greenhouse of the furrow type

Two or more A-frame greenhouses connected along the eave length are used for designs of this kind. The eave acts as a gutter or furrow to take away rain and melting snow. The sidewall is removed between the greenhouses, resulting in a single expansive interior, interior space consolidation that eliminates labor, lowers automation costs, increases personal management, and decreases fuel consumption. There is less exposed wall area from which heat escapes. The snow loads must be included in these greenhouses' frame requirements because, as in the case of individual freestanding conservatories, the snow does not fall off the roofs but melts away. Despite the snow loads, in northern countries of Europe and Canada, ridge and furrow greenhouses are used successfully and are well suited to Indian conditions.

Saw Tooth and Quonset Type Greenhouse

Except that there is provision for natural ventilation in this form, these are almost comparable to ridge and furrow style greenhouses. In a saw-tooth style greenhouse, a particular natural ventilation flow path emerges.

CHAPTER 3

Overview of Different Types of Greenhouses

There are several types of greenhouses and their classifications are based on several factors. There are greenhouses that are classified by the materials that are used, greenhouses classified in accordance to technology, and many other classifications.

Low Technology Greenhouses

Low technology greenhouses are extensively used because of their tiny structures. They are typically three meters in height and have very less ventilation. They are the most inexpensive forms of greenhouses. These are typically used by small farmers and households to protect their plants. The provide facilities like warmer temperature, reduction in pests, and so on. They use very little technology and hence are easy to set up. These are most prominently found in places like Australia. The major problem with this kind is the lack of scope to optimize production due to low levels of technology. These types of greenhouses are usually dome structured.

Medium Technology Greenhouses

Medium level greenhouses are those that have a distinct division between the wall and floor. They aren't very big and are usually about 5.5 meters tall. They have better ventilation facilities and use medium levels of technology. Medium level greenhouses have glass walls or double plastic walls and are slightly more expensive than low technology greenhouses. These kinds of greenhouses are able to generate higher yields and have good usage of water. They eradicate disease-causing pests. However, the major problem with this kind of greenhouse is the lack of temperature regulation. Another issue is that the greenhouse does little to optimize production.

High Technology Greenhouses

High-level greenhouses are those that make use of high levels of technology. They are generally a lot taller and are about 8 meters high. These greenhouses optimize production. They have both wall and roof ventilation. With these greenhouses, temperature control is easy and can be regulated to suit crop needs. They are expensive. These greenhouses reduce the amount of pesticides used and at the same time eradicate pests much more than other greenhouses. The produce produced by the plants grown in high-technology greenhouses is fresh and of superior quality.

High Tunnel Greenhouse

High tunnels greenhouses are most commonly referred to as hoop greenhouses. They are usually made up of polyethylene fabric or a greenhouse film. They are very simple and are considered to be economically viable. This type of greenhouse allows the person to grow plants and these plants have optimum produce and prolong the growth season of the plant. They are extensively used in Europe and the Middle East. They are usually used as temporary filaments and use low levels of technology.

Industrial Greenhouse

An industrial greenhouse is highly technological driven greenhouses that are extensively used for commercial purposes. They cover vast areas of the land and are associated with industrial scale production. They are extremely expensive and specific in nature. They come with several facilities including huge amounts of vents, sunlight filters, and irrigation facilities, and so on. They are extensively used in companies which produce huge amounts of flowers for decorative purposes, farming companies, and so on. With this type of greenhouse, temperature control is very easy as the temperature can shuttle between cold and hot. This type optimizes production and yield and reduces pests by a huge amount.

Rooftop Greenhouse

Rooftop greenhouses are medium level technological greenhouses that are specifically suited to urban areas where the problem of space arises. This type of greenhouse is largely ventilated, providing enough sunlight and good temperature conditions for the person. The plants usually have a larger yield. This type of greenhouse blends the usage of natural sources as well as manmade sources. For instance, the original greenhouse keeps the plants warm during the day and cold during the night, this is a fluctuation that can cause damage to the plants. Rooftop greenhouses prevent this due to the existence of a thermal mass.

Commercial Greenhouse

Commercial greenhouses are not used by amateurs and are professional greenhouses built to suit the needs of commercial industries. They are very expensive and have customizable features. They are specially designed, keeping the needs of the company. Thus, they are highly technology driven and have several features like irrigation facilities, seed dispersion, storage, sunlight filters, and so on. They provide the most optimum production and eradicate pests.

Heated Greenhouse

Heated greenhouses have high levels of technology and are usually expensive. They are specific in nature because they cater only to the plants that grow in the summer but need to be cultivated in the winter. Heated greenhouses are extensively used on professional levels as well as in the amateur levels. There are several subdivisions in this type of greenhouse. They provide optimum production and have large vents and many at times contain valves that can regulate the heat generated in the greenhouses.

Insulated Greenhouse

Insulated greenhouses are extensively used in areas where there are erratic climatic conditions. With these types of greenhouses, the temperature can be controlled and regulated to allow the plants grow at their speed without the hindrance of spells of showers, heat, and other climatic fluctuations. These are extensively used by wealthier farmers for they are extremely expensive and require a large investment. These types of greenhouses are also the type that makes use of high-level technology.

Modular Greenhouse

Modular greenhouses are specially designed to provide a platform to grow multiple crops in a small storage space. They are used by gardeners and farmers who want to expand their production but often can't because of limited space. Modular greenhouses have several shelves and occupy less space. They also have several pockets and layers to grow plants on. They are mainly technologically driven and are expensive. These types of greenhouses have perforations in their layers to allow the sunlight to go to the bottom layer and so on. Though they are pricey, they reduce the overall cost because they enable people to expand plant growth without having to invest in another greenhouse.

CHAPTER 4
Planning Your Greenhouse

Location

The location of your greenhouse also depends on many factors. The first factor is the type of plant you want to grow inside your greenhouse. Tropical plants need maximum sunlight exposure so you must choose a greenhouse where sunlight comes in an appropriate amount. Most houseplants and flowers need good exposure to sunlight but not direct. Your location also depends on the climate of your area. If you live in a warm place, then you must need proper shading for your greenhouse. However, if you live in a cold area then you need maximum exposure of sunlight. Remember that the sun changes its position in different seasons. A very sunny spot in June should not get any sun exposure during January season and you must consider this fact before choosing your greenhouse location.

Floor

You have a choice of what kind of floor or base you want for your greenhouse. Many people don't bother to cover their greenhouse base and they generally have mud or another floor where they constructed their greenhouse. This gives a natural look to your greenhouse. But it is not advisable to keep your floor open because many insects, worms, and rodents may grow inside the mud and should harm your plants. Some base constructions are available with the greenhouse construction kit and you don't need to buy extra material for your base. But if it is not available in your kit, you can buy it from the market. Concrete floors are a good option for your greenhouse's base as they make the best place to put your benches and other materials. Sometimes, wooden floors are also good for your greenhouse

Foundation

When you are building a greenhouse, the first step is to build a foundation. This needs to be done properly for you to have a solid greenhouse that will stand the test of time.

Whatever you decide to make your foundation out of, it needs to be both level and square. It needs to be big enough for the outside dimensions of the greenhouse to ensure it fits properly and can be secured.

You can buy pre-made greenhouse bases, and these are worth considering, but just be aware that these still need a flat and level surface to be installed on and will still need a foundation beneath them.

When building your greenhouse base, you can either make it out of poured concrete, or you can use sand and paving stones. Both are suitable and do the job well, though the latter has the advantage of being moveable in the future if necessary.

Ensure that not only are the edges of your base square but also that the diagonal measurements between the corners are also identical.

Under the base, you will need the foundation which is what supports the weight of the greenhouse, which it is secured to and prevents damage in windy weather.

If you live in an area where the ground freezes then your greenhouse foundation needs to be below the frost line. This is to prevent damage to your structure from the ground heaving as it freezes and melts. Your local Building Permit Agency will be able to tell you where the frost line is in your area. In warmer areas, this is only going to be a couple of inches at most, but in the colder, northern areas it can be as much as a few feet.

One good way of insulating your foundation and protecting it is to use 1" foam insulation. Put this down to your frost line to reduce heat loss through the soil, which has the benefit of reducing your heating costs.

The foundation is essential because this is what you are securing your greenhouse too. It will prevent weather damage and warping in hot or cold weather. If you do not secure your greenhouse properly, then don't expect it to last the growing season. If the greenhouse starts to warp, then you can find your panes shatter or crack and become very hard to re-fit. You can also find doors and windows become stiff and very difficult to use too.

If you have bought a new greenhouse, then any warranty will not cover damage due to not having a proper greenhouse base.

Your greenhouse is built on this foundation and base, which will ensure it, is easier to erect and that it will last.

There are some different choices for the foundation, which we'll discuss now.

Compacted Soil

If you compact the soil enough, then you can build your greenhouse directly on the ground, particularly if you live in an area where the ground doesn't freeze too badly.

A lot of greenhouses will come with an optional metal plinth that has spikes in each corner. These can be cemented into the ground to prevent the base from moving.

You will still need to level the ground though, so dig out your spirit level. It is best to use a roller or other mechanical device to compact the soil to ensure it is stable. Do not build your base out of gravel or hardcore because these are just not stable enough.

The advantage of using the soil as your foundation is that it is very cost-effective. You can also use the existing ground for growing your plants in plus drainage is a lot better.

The downside of soil is that it will allow pests into your greenhouse. You will find this particularly bad in winter as pests flock to your greenhouse for the warmth.

Perimeter Bases

This is a slightly cheaper option where you use bricks, breeze blocks or thin paving or edging slabs to create a foundation directly under the greenhouse frame. You can use concrete if you prefer.

The foundation is built along where the frame will run, leaving the soil in the middle of the greenhouse untouched.

While you can build the foundation directly on the soil, most people will cut out a trench and place the foundation in the trench. The advantage of this latter approach is that it is easier to level.

Slabs or Paving

This is a very popular way to build your greenhouse foundation because it keeps out the weeds and pests while giving you a good, clean growing environment.

This method involves building a base the size of your greenhouse out of paving slabs and then fixing your greenhouse to it. This type of base will last for many years and is very low maintenance.

You can screw your greenhouse to the base to provide stability in windy conditions, preventing any damage. It also provides good drainage when compared to an all-concrete base.

In the winter months, a soil floor can get damp and encourage mold to grow. A paved floor helps to keep the greenhouse both warmer and drier in the cooler months.

Providing you bed down the slabs properly with an inch or two of sand underneath them they are surprisingly easy to get level and will not warp or move over time.

Concrete Base

This is where you mark out where your greenhouse will be and dig down a few inches before pouring concrete in to form the base.

For larger greenhouses, this has its advantages, but it can be expensive and does require special tools such as a concrete mixer.

This is a very durable base, and you can fit expansion bolts to secure larger structures. You may have an issue with standing water so you may want to consider putting drainage holes in to prevent standing water.

Frame

The frame is extremely important, because it provides the integrity of the structure, and also anchors the greenhouse covering.

The materials available for frames are:

Aluminum

This will provide a very strong frame that does not rust, and it's lightweight. It has a very long lifespan and it's the most widely used frame for greenhouses. Aluminum has extruding channels, which are perfect for inserting the covering panels.

Steel

Steel that is galvanized is a very strong and long-lasting plus, it's reasonably priced. Because of its strength, you require just a little for the framing, which adds the amount of light passing on to the plants.

Steel is also very heavy and ensures the greenhouse remains solid no matter the weather conditions or temperature levels. However, the transportation and assembling of the greenhouse can be difficult since the steel is heavy.

Plastic Resin

These are very attractive and are very popular. This is because, compared to aluminum, they are less expensive, and they also do not conduct any heat away from the greenhouse-like steel does.

Unfortunately, they lack the strength of the metal frames, and can only be used for the smaller greenhouses, with shorter dimensions. They can only be used with polycarbonate panels.

Wood

Wooden frames are ideal for a simple do-it-yourself greenhouse project. Wood is beautiful and provides sufficient durability and strength but it is susceptible to rotting, therefore don't allow contact with moisture.

Glazing

Tempered Glass

These are strong and impact-resistant. This means that they will withstand any expansions or contractions during the seasonal temperature changes. The 3mm single pane thickness is ideal for the greenhouse.

However, the 4mm thickness is much stronger and will provide additional insulation. You must protect the hedges during insulation, as the glass may shatter if hit hard. Tempered glass is much more expensive compared to the polycarbonate panels.

Tempered glass is more durable even if it's expensive, and it is more resistant to scratches, as well as being very clear and providing no diffusion.

Fiberglass

This is translucent and provides a light that is well-diffused. Fiberglass retains heat better than normal glass. The greenhouses made from fiberglass are normally corrugated to provide adequate rigidity because the outer coat will become sunbaked within 6-10 years. The surface will become etched and yellow.

Polycarbonate

It is UV treated, lightweight and durable. It is high quality and modern material used for greenhouses. The polycarbonate is available in different levels of thickness and provides the clarity of glass, but it's not scratch resistant, or as strong as the tempered glass.

The single-walled one does not retain any heat and provides no light diffusion. It, however, has a longer lifespan of more than 15 years, depending on the region.

Twin-Walled Polycarbonate

This is very popular because it has internal spaces providing strength and excellent insulation. The best point to note about the twin-walled polycarbonate is that it diffuses light.

Triple-Walled Polycarbonate

This is similar to twin-walled polycarbonate, but it has extra strength and heat retention abilities. In cold climates, the triple-walled polycarbonate is extremely useful for all-year-round indoor gardening, because it will withstand snow loads and will freeze without cracking or distorting.

Securing against the Wind

Any surface such as a wall, fence, or even nearby buildings can act as protection against gusts of wind or even snow. When plants are close to these surfaces, they can leech onto the small amount of warmth that they provide. During summer, if your plants cannot stand the heat, you can use these surfaces as sun blocks.

There are a lot of considerations to be made before you buy a greenhouse. Obviously, there is budget, but other factors may well influence your budget. If you live in a particularly cold area, then double glazing and heating are important, but in a hotter area, the primary considerations would be air flow and ventilation.

CHAPTER 5

Constructing a Greenhouse

Now that you understand what a greenhouse is and what you need to get started with planting, you need to know what materials you need to build your greenhouse. This sounds like a massive feat, and in some respects, it is. Depending on the size and style of the greenhouse you want this can either be a really hard part of the job or a really easy part of the job?

DIY

1. You need to first choose what kind of greenhouse you want to build. This includes the style and the frame of your greenhouse. There are dozens upon dozens of types of greenhouses, and you must decide which one will suit your needs best. There is no point in creating a budget for yourself until you've chosen what type of greenhouse because this can impact the cost of the building.

2. Once you have a clear image of what you want your greenhouse to look like, you want to make sure that it is functional and long-lasting. Sometimes you might even want it to look a specific way. That's okay. This is where you get to have fun and customize your greenhouse to you. You get to choose the type of doors you want in your greenhouse and the hardware that is used to build it. A word of caution: make sure that the doors are quality and well-insulated

because you don't want them messing with your greenhouse climate. The hardware side of things means the type of material you are going to have held your greenhouse in one piece. Any greenhouse you build needs to have all the correct brackets, bolts, and other hardware items to ensure that it remains together no matter the weather outside.

3. You need to decide what coverage you are going to go with next. Your budget and greenhouse needs will play a role in what type of covering you choose. They can vary in thickness and material type. However, keep in mind your covering needs to be durable for all weather conditions. You don't want extreme winds to tear into your covering. You can install this on your own if you choose, or you can have someone do it for you.

4. When it comes to building a greenhouse, you cannot skip out on things such as ventilation or cooling systems. Your ventilation system should probably cool your greenhouse so that your plants don't overheat from excessive levels of heat. You could even try and use shading to your best advantage to cool your greenhouse down. Your ventilation needs will vary depending on the size of your greenhouse.

5. Once you have ventilation picked out you need to decide on what type of heating system you are going to use. Climate control is about more than merely cooling things down. Your heating option might be using natural gas, oil heaters, water heaters, propane heaters, convection tubing, or any of the other various heating methods employed in greenhouses. It's up to you to decide which one matches your budget and your routine.

6. You already know that maintaining control over the heating and cooling in your greenhouse is essential to providing your plants with the proper climate that they require. You want your greenhouse to be energy-efficient in a perfect world but also for it to be functional. You can use a thermostat or even computer programs to help you maintain control of your greenhouse climate. Greenhouse climate controls are normally very user-friendly so you shouldn't have to worry about it being over complicated. Make sure you choose the right environmental control regulator to suit your needs and expertise level.

7. As a newbie when it comes to greenhouses, there's a lot to keep in mind. You ultimately have to decide what is worthwhile to have with you when you start in your greenhouse — don't worry, mistakes can be corrected at later

dates. Some of the things that can help a novice in the field of greenhouse gardening are items like a CO_2 generator and irrigation systems. The CO_2 generator will make sure your plants are getting what they need to maintain their growth. Having a system to irrigate your plants can ensure they get their needed water (however, you can also do this by hand if you prefer). There are lots of different systems out there to help you maintain perfect conditions in a greenhouse, but they are not all necessary for your specific needs. Weed out the ones you need from the ones you don't to minimize your costs.

8. You might not immediately think about benches in your greenhouse; however, they are a nice added feature that provides you comfort in your greenhouse. Benching can be used to store your plants, or even for you to have a place to sit in your greenhouse.

9. Once you know everything that you need and want for your greenhouse it's time to place an order for the materials. You can either do this yourself or have it delivered for you to build or you can order them through a company that will come and set the greenhouse up for you.

10. When you're all done you go ahead and build your greenhouse. It is useful to buy all your materials from one place because they can often provide you with instruction manuals on your build to better assist you in putting the greenhouse together.

Side note: Before adding a greenhouse to your property make sure that you have consent to build from any local authorities that you need it from and that you understand the possible tax implications it may or may not have for you.

Greenhouse Kits

Do you use a kit from a company or do you build it all yourself from start to finish? While the greenhouse kit might seem higher in price than doing it all yourself, you might be saving yourself time and money in the long run by having everything you need in front of you with a map to put it together.

This ultimately comes down to your expertise in building and your comfort level ensuring that everything is put together correctly for your greenhouse.

I cannot stress enough how important it is to make sure that both your ventilation and heating systems are up to par and working as they should be. You want to regulate the temperature in your greenhouse which means that you need to make sure that your ventilation system can release the excess heat and moisture before it destroys your crop.

The roof provides its series of issues to be concerned about. Most greenhouses have peaked roofs and this is for a variety of reasons. However, for those that live in snowy climates, the main reason is so that the snow doesn't gather and collapse your roof. You can combat this if you choose to go for other roof styles such as the dome. You merely need to make sure that there is plenty of pitch on the roof to prevent snow and ice from collecting all in one area.

Flooring is another aspect of your greenhouse. Do you see where every aspect of your greenhouse can be personally tailored to your preferences? While gravel flooring is best for beginners since it is low maintenance and provides great and simple drainage, some people prefer to use concrete tiling in their greenhouses.

Finally, you need to think about how you are going to get the sun's rays into your greenhouse and to your plants. There is a wide range of materials that you can use for greenhouse windows, doors, and roofs. For example, there is glass, polycarbonate, and plastic sheeting specifically designed for greenhouses.

Used Greenhouse

Greenhouse expansion is not as uncommon as you might initially think it is. Often new growers get the hang of what they are doing, and their greenhouse space quickly becomes too small for their needs. If you're feeding your family or a community with your greenhouse then over time you might want to have more space to include a wider variety of fruits and vegetables. Sometimes the expansion of your greenhouse goes beyond simply making a few spacing adjustments and you end up needing to physically expand it.

First, establish what size you want your expanded greenhouse to be. Keep in mind that this might not be the last time you have your greenhouse expanded so please be aware of that and keep space allotted for potential growth in the future. It helps to build your greenhouse expansion slightly bigger than what you think you will need at this moment. This allows you space for future growth within your greenhouse as well and prolongs the time between possible greenhouse expansions.

When you look at space and size, you also need to plan for the best outcome for your plant's growth. This means that you want to ensure your greenhouse is running at its best climate levels to continue with the proper production of your crops. This is where you consider all the extra systems like vents, ventilation systems, material types, style and build of the greenhouse to promote the environment you want inside for your plants.

It's great to think about expansion in terms of what we are bringing in that is new to the scene, however, you must also bear in mind what you already have and what to do with those items. Some of the systems you have in place for your greenhouse will still be sufficient to run and protect your plants even with the expansion. Other systems might need to be updated, replaced, or duplicated to maintain the proper climate for your old plants and the new ones coming in. Get a second opinion because this is where your expansion can become costly and you want to make sure that you are doing it the right way.

There's a lot to consider and do before physically expanding your greenhouse. Part of that is double-checking the regulations of where you live. Sometimes you might need to speak to a building inspector or get another permit to build for the expansion. You don't want to expand and unknowingly break any laws that force you to tear down all of your hard work. So, acquaint yourself with all regulations about your greenhouse building and plan accordingly.

The other caveat is that with an expansion you need to keep in mind you will produce a bigger yield.

CHAPTER 6

How to save money by building your greenhouse

Did you know that gardening is not only a great source of enjoyment as a hobby but also a great way to save money?

Well, it is true that first you have to invest a little bit in your garden. However, in about a year it will start to pay off in produce. Let us learn some ways to save money while gardening.

The first and most obvious way that you will save money is by growing your own food. You will go out into the garden to harvest what will become about half of your lunch, and you can preserve the surplus for use later in the year. By harvesting half of your lunch, you will be able to save between $5 to $10 a day between the middle of July to the middle of September.

This represents what it would cost you to purchase your lunch while you are at work. Your weekly savings will be about $25 to $50. Conservatively, over a 10-week period, you will be able to save between $250 and $500, even with a small urban garden. If you have little space, you can concentrate on crops that are either not available in your area or that are very expensive to purchase at the store.

For the plants in your garden to produce food for you, they need nutrients. If you rely on store-bought products, that can be a continued cost to your garden.

You can evaluate several free and local resources for their fertilizer potential; these resources are either produced in your yard, such as autumn leaves, or in your kitchen, such as spent coffee grounds or used tea leaves (if used to make compost or mulch). They give back their nutrients in the garden, fertilizing your plants freely. Then you do not have to purchase any store-bought fertilizers for your garden. This will save you the cost of the fertilizer. The free and local resources that you can use in the garden you can take from the landfill. If you are a beginner, you can save money by filling your garden with compost made from these free and local resources instead of purchasing it from a garden center.

Collecting rainwater is another great way to save some money during the summer. If it is not raining enough, then you need to water your garden. Typically, when the garden needs supplemental water, prices jump because there is more demand on the municipal system in the summer. Your bill can increase by as much as $60 a month during dry weather simply because you are watering your garden. You can have rain barrels that have more than enough capacity to capture and store water to get through the drier times.

If you have another dry summer, these rain barrels can save you up to $360 while reducing the likelihood that you will lose plants due to drought. If it is not raining and your rain barrels are not full, you can recycle water from your kitchen, from things like washing vegetables, boiling water, and many other sources, and then use it directly in the garden.

You can save money by saving seeds. Saving seeds and participating in seed exchanges can build you a large seeds library that often does not have to cost very much. Once you have your seeds, you can often start your own seedlings for a fraction of the cost of purchasing them. If you have a south- or southwest-facing window, you can use the seeds that you have saved in the garden along with recycled containers filled with bulk potting soil to start your own seedlings for pennies. Seedlings in the garden store are not usually very expensive but when you think about how many plants it takes to fill a garden, those savings can really add up.

When you go into a garden center, invest in perennials that will produce crops for you. Look for crops that you cannot find here or focus on the more costly crops that your family eats a lot. Perennials that produce crops are a great investment; as you need to invest only once and the crops will produce often for decades, paying themselves off many times over. If you would like to stretch your investment, you can propagate perennials. Propagation does not have to cost a lot and there are even some perennials, such as raspberries and strawberries, which self-propagate if you give them the space; they will produce massive crops for you with very little effort. Once you have your crops, you can increase their value by processing them into something that will cost you more at the grocery store, such as grapes, rhubarb, and surplus berries.

You can also recover the value from crops that may not be fresh enough for other purposes but that are not quite rotting by turning them into wine. Each batch of wine costs about $10 to make and yields 30 standard bottles. At the store, each bottle of wine would cost a minimum of $10. By making these crops into wine, each batch increases the value of the crop by around $290.

Initially, landscaping the garden is often the most costly part of gardening. You can use naturally sourced materials such as stone but you will need to invest in other things. When you have to purchase materials for projects, you can calculate— before you start the project—when it will pay off in either produce or savings. The rain barrels, for instance, will pay themselves off in one year as soon as there is a drought condition, whereas some of the other projects, such as perennials, may take a few more years, but eventually they will pay themselves off. Then you have the construction and expansion phase of your garden, which is a more expensive phase than the maintenance phase each subsequent year. However, once it is done, it will be much cheaper. The garden will continue to pay you back in produce and savings. In fact, the garden will increase how much it pays you back as your perennials mature and produce larger and larger crops.

CHAPTER 7
Creating the greenhouse environment

Once you've set up your greenhouse, it's time to do what it was supposed to do-foster quick and safe plant growth within it. A greenhouse's strength lies in the ability to control indoor climate conditions.

Temperature is one of those essential climatic conditions. If you want to achieve optimum plant growth, you need to have the right temperature. Light is another significant factor. Remember that one climate factor can influence another. For example, too much sunlight can increase the indoor temperature beyond the appropriate levels inside the greenhouse.

Heat

If the winters in your area are on the harsh side, or if you want to get a head start on seed germination before spring, you will need to consider adding in heating for your greenhouse.

Electrical heaters today are a lot more energy efficient than they used to be. The most important thing when it comes to choosing your heater is that it should have a thermostat – this helps to keep the temperature constant and makes the whole system more energy-efficient as the heater is turned off when the desired temperature has been reached.

There are several different types of heaters that you can get that are suited to greenhouses. Tubular heaters, fan heaters, and warming cables are all options to consider.

Ventilation

With two forms of ventilation in mind, each greenhouse should be built-natural and artificial ventilation. For natural ventilation, only a number of outlets and inlets need to be properly positioned to allow natural airflow into and out of the greenhouse. Electricity may or may not be used, but it would only be used to control inlets or outlets opening and closing. Although natural ventilation is a great cost saver, in areas with high outdoor temperatures, it is inefficient.

And that's where there's automatic ventilation. Auto ventilation controls indoor temperatures with louvers and exhaust fans powered by electricity. The distinction between automatic ventilation and natural ventilation powered by electricity is that the former is typically part of a larger air conditioning system that senses temperature and allows the louvers and fans to do so.

Cooling-A different approach is required when ventilation alone is inadequate to manage the temperature within the greenhouse. Two common thermal control strategies that can increase ventilation are fog systems and pad-and-fan systems.

To spread a cooling' fog' uniformly, fog systems use nozzles mounted every 50 to 100 feet in the greenhouse. It is expensive because it is necessary to use clean water to prevent blocking the tiny mouth of each nozzle.

For automatic ventilation, pad-and-fan technology goes hand in hand. For air inlets, evaporative pads are installed, and the air entering the greenhouse is cooled. In the end, the cool air circulates within the greenhouse, collecting heat before the exhaust fans take it out.

Without proper ventilation and air circulation, your plants are more vulnerable to attack by fungus and mold. You should only cut off the air supply in the very coldest of weather.

Air circulation helps to keep the temperature in the room constant in summer and prevents your plants from being stifled.

The general rule is that you need at least two ventilators for every 6 feet in length.

Greenhouse Ventilation Why It Important

To order to create an optimal atmosphere, a number of factors must be addressed in your greenhouse. One of the most important climatic variables is air quality. But you might wonder, "Why is my greenhouse ventilation so important?" There are a number of reasons for this. The plants will not grow as fast without proper ventilation, and what they produce will be inferior. Proper ventilation can help to keep your greenhouse climate at a degree that is best suited to the plants you cultivate.

Ventilation greatly affects environmental conditions in your greenhouse. Such factors affect the ability of the plant to perform photosynthesis. This process involves the ability of the plant to transform sunlight into chemical energy. The plant uses this energy to provide it with fuel to grow. This includes the ability of the plant to take important elements from the soil and complete the cycle of reproduction.

Proper greenhouse ventilation will help control the circulation of air, temperature, and humidity. These are factors affect the situation significantly plants ' ability to grow in a productive way. This will help to provide the required amount of carbon dioxide for your plants to grow.

In order to produce such photosynthesis, plants need carbon dioxide to perform proper chemical reactions. As carbon dioxide levels begin to decrease the plant's ability to grow, they decrease. Proper ventilation in your greenhouse can help to keep carbon dioxide levels at the amount needed to grow healthily.

We absorb carbon dioxide as the plants grow and produce oxygen. But many people do not know that oxygen is required for plants to grow. Their roots require oxygen from the fresh air. The roots need oxygen to expand, and this is directly related to the ability of the plant to take nutrients from the soil.

Humidity

Humidity here refers to the amount of moisture in the greenhouse growing environment. It is no news that keeping the wrong humidity in the greenhouse is detrimental to the growth of the plants. Here are a few tips on how to maintain the right relative humidity:

1. Avoid overwatering your growing medium. Too much watering is the beginning of trouble in the plants' root system. The humidity level in the

greenhouse increases when there is too much water in the medium.

2. Ensure enough air circulation. This will improve the ventilation in the greenhouse and invariably ensure the right humidity level.

To keep plants from succumbing to disease, humidity must be kept in check. High humidity content in greenhouse air increases plant condensation, hampering breathing. Moreover, high humidity is a breeding ground for rodents and fungal diseases of plants. The vapor pressure deficit (VPD) must be routinely measured and maintained at the optimum level of 0 to 1 psi for better management of humidity. VPD is an ambient humidity measure as opposed to the humidity at which water condensation starts.

Shade

Shading is a temperature and light control device that uses shades or blinders that are automatically operated. The curtains close when there is too much sunshine during the day or when it is required to maintain warm temperatures at night in the greenhouse. An internal temperature sensor detects and triggers the opening or closing of the shades.

The sun in summer can really scorch your plants, especially in a greenhouse. It is advisable to have shades fitted to the outside that can be easily rolled into place as necessary.

Benches: Not only provide the extra spacing in which you need to work, but they can also prevent you from bending too much. Looking for a ventilated shelving system that provides good drainage of water and circulation of air is a good idea.

Specifically, lights are required to provide your plants with photosynthesis up to 24 hours a day. Now, what's a greenhouse point if you don't have the winter option to grow seasonal veggies? Look at the latest fluorescent light designs that have recently reached the famous HID lamps.

While it is smart for all greenhouses to employ screens or shade cloth to reduce the heating impact of sunlight, it is absolutely critical for a free standing greenhouse. A free standing greenhouse is usually a large structure, so it takes longer for the heat to build up to a damaging level. However, because it is so large and the air mass inside is so hard to move, it takes much longer to evacuate that heat to safe levels.

A shade cloth or screen will block a certain amount of light from entering. This limits catastrophic heating, while also protecting the leaves of tender seedling from sun scald.

Shade cloths come in different densities that block different amounts of light. A shade cloth with a 40 percent density, blocks 40 percent of the light. A shade cloth with a 60 percent density blocks 60 percent of the light. I personally prefer a white shade cloth with around a 40 percent density. If you are buying a free standing greenhouse as a kit from a greenhouse supply, they will usually recommend the correct shade cloth density needed for that particular design.

Shade Cloth is usually made of polyethylene covered by UV and helps with heating and condensation. They can all be cut to suit your greenhouse practice.

Min / Max Thermometers: Measure both indoor and outdoor highs and lows. But what's important about these thermometers is it will provide you with valuable information about how a given day's temperature fluctuates. This alone will tell you in your greenhouse if you need additional cooling or heating elements that can help you with your budget.

Watering systems have several different services, primarily to help with plant growth, cooling, and moisture. Depending on the type of greenhouse you want, you usually want to keep the humidity around 60%.

You might want to invest in these for little more complicated greenhouses: when you're home, thermostats will support your greenhouse. Place a thermostat right in the middle of your greenhouse if you want to keep a worry-free temperature in your greenhouse. You would like to have a thermostat of heating and cooling close together and away from the sunlight, if possible.

If you are in cold climates, heaters are critical. Even if heat comes from sunlight during the day and is trapped in a greenhouse, it may not be enough. There are plenty of choices from electric heaters to gas heaters.

Evaporative Air Coolers are the best greenhouse cooling systems out there and usually come with a thermostat-built system. Water flows onto cooling pads, which reduces the circulating air temperature. Another useful feature is that they help filter bugs and dirt.

Lighting

While your electrician is fitting the heaters, it makes sense for them to also fit lights for the greenhouse. The type of light will depend on what the purpose of the light is.

You can make the space more aesthetically appealing by spotlighting particular areas in the greenhouse or more practical by adding in strip lighting.

Again, you should not place the lights too close to the actual plants. A ultra-violet lamp can also be installed to provide better lighting in low-light conditions.

LED lighting is more expensive to install upfront but a lot more energy efficient than the incandescent bulbs or even your energy-saver bulbs.

It is also a good idea to place the light switches close to the entrance of the greenhouse so that you can find them easily in the dark.

Irrigation

If your greenhouse is in your garden then it is easy enough to pop down and water it, but if it is at an allotment or you are on holiday then watering becomes much trickier, putting your harvest at risk.

In the hottest weather, and more so in hotter climates, you will need to water your plants two or three times a day to keep them healthy no matter how good your cooling system is!

CHAPTER 8

Essential Greenhouse Equipment

As it's been said, a business can never prevail without the correct instruments and gadgets that will help or help the business person in dealing with the business.

Thinking about the idea of business greenhouses, it is critical to acquire the correct equipment so as to give the important necessities of the plants.

For the individuals who are intending to build up a business greenhouse, here is a rundown of a portion of the equipment that you should have:

1. Business greenhouse warmers

Like any kind of greenhouse, regardless of whether individual or business, radiators are viewed as one of the most significant equipment. This is particularly helpful and valuable throughout the winter season, where producing heat inside the greenhouse is alongside unimaginable.

So as to benefit from your pay potential regardless of whether it is as of now winter, attempt to get the best business greenhouse haters. This will bait your plants to keep creating more and, thus, will give you a lasting through the year benefit.

2. Hard-wearing, profoundly strong greenhouse organizing

Since you will deliver more vegetation or posterity contrasted with different greenhouses that are just worked for joy or relaxation, it is essential to get a greenhouse organizing that is rock solid and hard wearing.

For example, the vast majority of your items are set in overwhelming pots, thus, so as to haul them around the greenhouse or moving them to your truck for conveyance, it is essential to utilize greenhouse organizing for simpler exchange.

3. Seed plate rack

In the event that your point is to deliver the same number of items in a year as you can, at that point you need to procure seed plate retires or racks. This will completely spare you more space inside the greenhouse. Right now, find a workable pace a lot of vegetation as you can without congestion your business greenhouse.

The more you can develop plants, the more benefit you can procure.

4. Watering equipment

The vast majority of the business greenhouses are bigger and greater than the normal greenhouses that can be found in one's patio. Henceforth, watering the plants can be monotonous. That is the reason it is significant that you get your nursery some watering equipment's that particularly intended to deal with the watering calendar of the plants.

5. Thermometers

Huge business greenhouses likewise need substantial thermometers. Regardless of whether the territory is so enormous, it is as yet critical to oversee and control the temperature inside the center.

Since it you are business greenhouse, it is difficult to screen temperature throughout the day. Subsequently, it is smarter to acquire and use the temperature of the greenhouse and simultaneously consequently opens a window to control the warmth inside the nursery. These sorts of business greenhouse thermometers are normally mounted to an uncommon gadget that mechanically opens a window once the temperature gets more sweltering than the necessary sum.

These are only a couple of the numerous business greenhouse equipment that you have to acquire so as to include a smooth stream inside your zone. In any case, these are a portion of the nuts and bolts so getting them would as of now guarantee you of an appropriate administration with your business greenhouse.

CHAPTER 9
Using Space Effectively

The major difference between traditional gardening and greenhouse gardening is that in greenhouse gardening, the growing environment is created by the grower. This means that the success of the greenhouse cultivation depends largely on the growing environment created.

If perhaps you are just starting out, it may seem confusing but if you focus on getting the basics right, you will realize that it is not as complex as it seems. In order to successfully cultivate plants using a greenhouse, you majorly need to focus on four basic aspects which are the soil, light, air and space.

You can choose to save yourself the stress of mixing your soil yourself and just purchase it or choose to do it yourself. Whichever your choice is, here is how to know the right potting soil to use for your greenhouse. The first thing to keep in mind is an understanding of what potting soil is. Potting soil is majorly a mixture of compost, peat moss and perlite or vermiculite.

These are usually the basic three, but there can be more substances added to the mixture in some other cases. The mixture ensures that the soil is able to hold nutrients and water and at the same time provide the plants with enough air. Good soil will comprise all the nutrients required by your plants for optimum growth, and also give sufficient aeration to the roots of the plants. Aeration is very important to the plant roots but so is water retention. Good soil must then be able to provide good aeration and at the same time be able to retain water. Contrary to what many new growers believe, the weight of potting soil is not the criteria to judge its quality. In other words, the weight of potting soil does not determine its quality. In fact, the weight is probably due to wetness or the presence of unnecessary sand which of course affects the quality of the potting soil. Good potting soil must be able to provide stability to the plants. When purchasing potting soil, there are some with the inscription 'slow release' or 'starter charge'. The ones that have starter charge inscribed on them simply mean that they have enough fertilizer in them to get the plants through the initial growth stage. After which you will need to add fertilizer by yourself to carry the plants through to their later growth stage. The potting soils that have slow release inscribed on them simply mean that they have fertilizer, a bit more than the starter charge, but will only be sufficient to carry the plants through for a few weeks. Some potting soils also have added substances that enable the soil to retain moisture more and therefore need less watering. Whichever potting soil you eventually purchase, you should remember to keep an eye on the features and consider if the features will suit the plant you intend to cultivate. However, there are certain situations where the basic potting soil mixture will not work effectively in the greenhouse as in the case of growing orchids. This is because orchids generally require a considerable amount of drainage and this requires a special kind of potting soil mixture. If you are mixing the soil yourself, ensure to sterilize your final mixture and consider the plants you are cultivating as you try out a good blend of different mixtures.

CHAPTER 10
What to plant in your greenhouse

Having a greenhouse can be the most satisfying thing that you have ever done. You can have one just about anywhere, in a city, a suburb, or on a farm. There are some pride and gratitude that come from watching seeds and cuttings grow into plants, and before you realize what happened, you have plants that will feed you and your family.

What Plants to Grow

The first thing you have to decide is what plants you want to grow and how many you want. If you are brand new to greenhouse gardening, you should probably begin with just one crop. If you begin growing an assortment of plants, it might be more than you can handle since each plant will have its own shade, fertilizing, spraying and watering requirement. You don't need all that hassle when you could just grow 10,000 of a specific plant just as easily as 3,000 plants of various types.

When you are trying to figure out what plants you want to grow, you need to know your ability to grow plants first. Then you have to figure out how many plants you are able to grow and how much it will cost you to grow the plants. Knowing how much it will cost to produce your plants will help you figure out which plants to grow.

Seed Starting and Propagation

Sowing Seeds

When you have figured out which plants you want to grow, you need to sow the seeds either in pots, boxes, or outside. If you are a new grower, begin putting them in pots. These are best for seeds that germinate slowly. It will be easy to see and get rid of weeds without bothering the seeds. The speed they will germinate depends on the amount of oxygen, moisture, and temperature they get. A seedbed in a shaded area will give them the best temperature because the hot sun could injure or kill the seedlings as they begin to grow. Make sure your soil is well-drained but stays moist to keep the oxygen levels stable. Having good air circulation around the seedlings will keep them from damping off.

The depth at which you sow the seeds will depend on how big they are. The best "rule of thumb" is to plant them at a depth that is three or four times larger than their diameter. If you have very tiny seeds, just sprinkle some on top of the dirt and cover them over lightly with more dirt. When they get large enough, you can transplant them into larger pots. This can "harden" the plant. This allows the plant to handle harsh weather conditions. Sow the seeds in either sand, peat moss, vermiculite, or a combination of these.

Your Greenhouse

The main purpose of having a greenhouse is to get your plants growing faster by keeping the temperature and humidity stable. You can also create the right temperature and light intensity for your crop. This is another good reason to think about growing huge quantities of just a few kinds of plants instead of trying to grow huge amounts of various plants. You shouldn't be scared of experimenting. During the first year of growing plants in a greenhouse, begin some plants in the late winter to have them ready by late spring or early summer. Test some different kinds during the first winter, where temperatures are below zero. This will help you learn more about your greenhouse and how much heat you will need to keep your plants alive.

As for your greenhouse, one that has been designed well and is covered with a double layer of poly will use about 50 percent less heat than a single layer, fiberglass house that most people use. A double poly greenhouse will last you for about four years; a single layer will last around six months. Newer greenhouses with inflated double poly plastic sheets won't cost as much as the polycarbonate, acrylic, and glass greenhouses.

Light Transmission

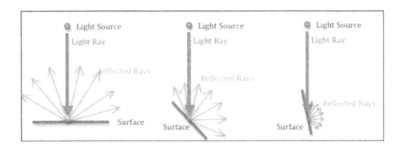

If you want to make sure your plants get the right amount of sun takes a lot of planning. This will include finding a way to get the best light during winter's cloudy and dark days. You need to stay away from too much light as this can kill your plants if you don't ventilate them properly.

This highest amount of sunlight, which ranges between 90 and 93 percent, can be provided by glass sheets. When the glass has been framed properly, the greenhouse won't be able to transmit more than 70 percent light. When you take into consideration the heating pipes, wiring, and other obstacles, this will lower your light transmission -down to 60 and 70 percent. You do have the choice of using double-poly sheeting or panels made from polycarbonate or acrylic. With some well-designed framing, you could get the same level of light that glass sheets can give you.

In order to figure out the amount of shade your plants are going to need, you could buy a light meter that can help you adjust it to the right degrees. These devices have a numbered guide that is easy to read. Just keep it away from direct sunlight. Keep it in the darker places of your greenhouse and then read the meter. Your readings might change depending on where the sun is located and any reflections.

Shades that you can place over the greenhouse or inside it that you can roll up and down when needed can help you regulate the amount of light your plants get. This cloth will cost you around ten cents per square foot and will last for ten years. When figuring out the amount of light you need to block out, the best choice would be about 65 to 73 percent for any type of foliage plant. Most growers will use 73 percent during the hot summer months and 55 percent during winter.

If you don't use the right amount of shade cloth, your plants could become too dry or sunburned. If you use too much shade, your plants will stay too wet, and this can lead to fungus or other diseases. The amount of shade depends on the plants that you are growing.

Most vegetable and flowering plants will do better during summer under some shade cloth, but you might not need shade during some of the other months. Some landscaping plants will grow great under some light shade. If you grow hanging plants, make sure you hang them between two and three feet apart. You could use between 55 to 75 percent shade. Most people don't realize that plants grown in the shade don't require any shade during the winter.

Shading paint is one more option. These compounds are painted on the outside of your poly-greenhouse cover. You can find several good ones at your local home improvement stores. If you can grow your plants under shade during the last part of their maturity, your plants will be of better quality. You can make a shade house from four by fours and two by fours.

You could use scrap lumber to create one. A cheap one can be made from some 12-foot pressure-treated poles, mobile home anchors, aircraft cables with clamps, and the right size cloth to cover the sides and top. You will set the 12-foot poles about 20 feet apart on each corner, or where you need the most strength. Then stretch the aircraft cable over the top and fasten it to the ground with the mobile home anchors. The entire structure gets covered with cloth, and then the sides and corners are stitched together.

Controlling the Environment

You just can't overestimate how important it is to control your greenhouse's environment. Moving, fresh air is just as crucial to the plants as water and light. It doesn't matter if you are growing your plants hydroponically or in pots; you have to watch the temperature. Temperatures need to stay around 70 to 75 degrees and the humidity needs to be at 50 percent. If you can keep these levels consistent, your plants will grow faster, have better color, and be of a higher quality.

If you can properly manage the climate inside the greenhouse, the production will normally be more than you ever imagined.

CO2

Everybody who has ever grown anything knows that carbon dioxide is needed for healthy plants. During the autumn and winter months, when you keep your greenhouse closed to keep it warmer, there won't be that much air circulation from outside. You can help your plants grow better by raising the CO2 levels. Normal concentrations are usually between 250 and 350 ppm. If you can raise the level to between 1200 and 1500 ppm could help your plants grow better. Enriching your plants with carbon dioxide won't replace your good growing skills.

Watering Your Plants

You need to feed your plants the right amount of water. If your plants get too dry, they will quit growing, and this could lead to stunting. You can stay away from this by testing your water for contaminants. This can be done by putting some water in a jar and taking it to your local county extension office to be tested. The first thing in the morning would be the best time. The best way to check for your pots' moisture level is to push your finger into the soil a few inches to see how moist the soil feels. Water the plants so that the soil becomes drenched in the pot. Add a water-soluble fertilizer to your plants once every ten days. Adding some peat moss to the soil will create a soil that holds water better and more constant.

Propagation

If you are growing your plants from seeds, make sure to transplant them when they become seedlings into rock wool, the ground, or a container. This propagation stage will have different requirements and demands for moisture and temperature. If you are growing cuttings, give them an environment that encourages rooting. The best method would be to take cuttings from your existing plants or to buy some. The best plants that grow the best from cuttings are herbs, flowers, foliage plants, shrubs, any type of vine, tomatoes, and cucumbers. Using a rooting hormone on the cuttings can help them take root faster.

Misting

Rooting your cuttings under a mist or spray is a technique that many greenhouse growers and beginners like using. The purpose of this is to keep a film of water on the plant's leaves; this will keep the cuttings strong until they grow enough roots. Once they have established roots, you can expose them to more air and light without hurting them.

Misting can speed up the rooting process, helps plants that are harder to root, and keep diseases away in cuttings by keeping all the fungus spores off the plant before they can attack the plant. Even though the leaves during this process have to be kept moist constantly, you need to keep the amount at a minimum. Too much water could leach out nutrients from the compost and could cause the plant to starve. Overwatering could harm the cutting, so make sure you use nozzles that can produce an extremely fine mist.

CHAPTER 11
Growing Vegetables, Herbs, and Fruits

HERBS

Herb gardens are hip and happening these days. Neighbors, companions, family... everyone has one. Regardless of whether you have a huge or a little nursery, there is constantly a spot where you can develop a few herbs. Be that as it may, how to begin? Beneath, you will discover 7 tips that will assist you with beginning with your herb garden.

1. Pick your preferred herbs

Before you start making your own herb garden, you ought to pick which herbs to develop. Pick the herbs that you like utilizing best. Consider which suppers you set up the most, and which fixings you requirement for those. Or on the other hand consider mixes of herbs that you can use in a summery mixed drink. For example, rosemary is tasty in a reviving Gin and Tonic. Be that as it may, hello, you didn't hear it from me.

On the off chance that you grow a variety of herbs immediately, it may become work serious. That is on the grounds that all herbs require a particular consideration routine, and before you realize it you're going through hours on them. So make a determination and spotlight on those. Achievement is ensured!

2. Keep your herbs inside from the start

In case you need to plant the herbs yourself, it's ideal to begin inside. Along these lines, the seeds will develop a lot quicker. Sow them in little window boxes and ensure that overabundance water can deplete. At the point when it quits freezing around evening time, you can steadily begin putting the plants outside. Put them out a little longer each time with the goal that they can become acclimated to the temperatures.

3. Try not to stand by too long to even think about transferring your herbs to a vegetable nursery box

On the off chance that you begin developing your herbs inside, don't stand by too long to even consider transferring them outside. In the event that you do, they will transform into long floppy stalks, attempting to develop towards the light. When the climate licenses, you ought to repot them to a grower or vegetable nursery box. Talking about which, those are additionally perfect for an overhang or porch. That way, you generally include your herbs inside reach. If there's a chance that the climate is awful, you can simply put them inside.

One thing you should focus on while picking a vegetable nursery box, is that you pick one that is made of maintainable materials that are impervious to wind and climate. It is ideal to pick one made of aluminum, a tropic wood type or weatherproof pine. That will guarantee that you can appreciate it for a considerable length of time without an excessive amount of upkeep. Progressively about picking the correct sort of wood.

4. Consolidate the correct herbs

Not all herbs require a similar consideration, which is the reason it is ideal to join herbs with a similar consideration routine in a similar grower or herb bed. Mediterranean herbs, for example, rosemary, thyme, lavender, oregano and sage appreciate full sun and not all that much water. Basil, chives and parsley, then again, favor drinking somewhat more.

5. Abstain from congesting, make herb beds

Do you like a crisp mint tea? Or on the other hand a serving of mixed greens with a new note? At that point you ought to unquestionably think about developing mint in your nursery. This herb is anything but difficult to develop; be that as it may, it has an inclination to congest. So unquestionably make sure to corral them with garden wood fringes so they don't begin developing in your neighbor's nursery too :-) you could likewise plant them in a vegetable nursery box or grower.

6. Sow or plant in columns

In case you want to purchase herbs in a nursery place, it is ideal to plant them straightforwardly in soil outside. In the event that the climate licenses, obviously. Plant them in lines, so you can cull any weeds developing between your plants rapidly and no problem at all. Does a similar while planting herbs? Work in columns and leave enough space between the seeds.

7. Save your herbs for the winter

Do you like cooking with herbs from your own nursery all through the winter? At that point make little packages of the herbs and hang them topsy turvy in a dry and warm region. At the point when they have dried, you can store them in a cool and dim spot, in a holder or resealable sack. Do you lean toward freezing your herbs? At that point save them in the cooler for a limit of a half year.

VEGETABLES

1. On the off chance that it's getting cold and you have tomatoes despite everything maturing on the vine — spare your tomatoes! Pull the plants up and bring them inside to a warm dry spot. Hang them up, and the tomatoes will mature on the vine.

2. Friend planting is a superb method to improve your nursery. A few plants renew supplements lost by another, and a few mixes successfully ward bugs off.

3. Paint the handles of your nurseries instruments a brilliant, shading other than green to assist you with discovering them among your plants. You can likewise save a letter drop in your nursery for simple instrument stockpiling.

4. Fertilizer needs time to coordinate and balance out in the dirt. Apply a little while before planting.

5. There is a simple method to blend fertilizer into your dirt without a great deal of overwhelming work: Spread the manure over your nursery in the pre-winter, after all the reaping is finished. Spread with a winter mulch, for example, roughage or cleaved leaves and let nature follow through to its logical end. By spring, the softening day off soil living beings will have worked the manure in for you.

6. Like vining vegetables, however you haven't got the room? Train your melons, squash, and cucumbers onto a vertical trellis or fence. Spares space and looks pretty as well.

7. Nursery vegetables that become over-ready are an obvious objective for certain irritations. Expel them as quickly as time permits to maintain a strategic distance from recognition.

8. Onions are prepared to collect when the tops have fallen over. Let the dirt dry out, collect, and store in a warm, dry, dull spot until the tops dry. Remove the foliage down to an inch, at that point store in a cool, dry territory.

9. Keep earth off lettuce and cabbage leaves when developing by spreading a 1-2 inch layer of mulch (untreated by pesticides or manures) around each plant. This additionally helps hold the weeds down.

10. When planting a blossom or vegetable transplant, store a bunch of manure into each opening. Fertilizer will give transplants an additional lift that endures all through the developing season.

11. Bugs can't stand plants, for example, garlic, onions, chives and chrysanthemums. Develop these plants around the nursery to help repulse creepy crawlies.

12. Milk containers, soft drink bottles and other plastic compartments make extraordinary small scale spreads to put over your plants and shield them from ice.

13. For simple peas, start them inside. The germination rate is far superior,

and the seedlings will be more advantageous and better ready to ward off nuisances and ailment.

14. Sound soil implies solid plants that are better ready to oppose nuisances and infection, diminishing the requirement for hurtful pesticides

15. Another motivation to utilize common and natural manures and soil corrections: worms love them! Night crawlers are amazingly advantageous in the vegetable nursery; expanding air space in the dirt and deserting worm castings. Do what you can to empower worms in your dirt.

16. Diatomaceous earth makes a superb natural bug spray — it is a rough white powder used to harm the fingernail skin, skin and joints of bugs. It likewise makes a superb slug obstruction.

FRUITS

Such huge numbers of various types of fruit are accessible, so how would you start to conclude which to develop? Start with quality. At the point when delicate berries are homegrown, they can be gathered when completely ready, stout, and sweet, without worry for transportation and perishability. The flavor is remarkable.

The measure of nursery space accessible will be another integral factor. Pick between developing little fruits (berries that develop on little plants, vines, or hedges) or bigger tree fruits. Start with effortlessly raised, space-productive little fruits, for example, strawberries, blackberries, and raspberries. In any case, on the off chance that you have a spot in your scene for a fruit tree or two, don't leave behind the chance. Search for simple consideration fruit trees or even nontraditional trees, for example, mulberries or crabapples.

Fruits that Grow on Trees

Conventional plantation trees, for example, apples, peaches, pears, and fruits require some information and thoughtfulness regarding fertilization, pruning, bother control, treating, and different sorts of care. To limit or wipe out splashing for illness, search for new ailment safe cultivars of apple trees.

Plant overshadows fruit trees, which remain little enough for you to pick the fruit starting from the earliest stage. This is a sheltered, simple approach to collect. You won't need to carry around stepping stools or parity on them while working. Another preferred position of smaller person fruit trees is they start to tolerate fruit a lot more youthful than full-size trees do. What's more, if your garden is little, a diminutive person tree, which occupies less room than its full-size partner, is a decent other option.

Have a go at growing a super-predominate peach tree in a pot. Super-midgets are extra-smaller than normal trees that may arrive at just around 5 feet tall. Albeit other fruit trees come as super-smaller people, peaches produce tasty fruit with just one tree and are extraordinary for apprentices. (Numerous other fruit trees require a second cultivar for fertilization.)

Plant your super-predominate peach tree in a 24-inch-wide tub with waste gaps in the base. Keep it damp, very much treated, and in a radiant area during the developing season. On the off chance that your tree doesn't prove to be fruitful the principal year, give it time. It might require one more year or two to begin its vocation. During winter in chilly atmospheres, store the tree, tub and all, in a cool however ensured area.

Utilize clingy red balls that look like apples for control of apple slimy parasites on apple and plum trees. Apple parasites are fly hatchlings that burrow into creating fruit, making it nauseating and unappetizing.

Apple parasite flies are effortlessly tricked, notwithstanding. In the event that you put out clingy red balls that take after apples (natively constructed or bought through a nursery supply index), the egg-laying females will be pulled in to the ball and stall out. (This will end their egg-laying vocation!) Hang at any rate one clingy red ball in a smaller person tree and at least six in bigger trees.

Use tree groups to find slithering irritations ascending fruit tree trunks. Clingy plastic groups will find ants conveying aphids and crawling caterpillars, for example, vagabond moths and codling moths.

CHAPTER 12

Scheduling plants for year-round growing

I f you've equipped your greenhouse to be a hothouse, you can use your space to grow year-round, which is fantastic! That means you'll be able to, if you like, do some crop rotation or succession planting, so that you don't always have the same things growing at the same time. You'll likely want to keep the foliage plants you've put so much effort into, but if you're growing vegetables, swap them out sometimes so you don't get bored with what you have.

Suitable for

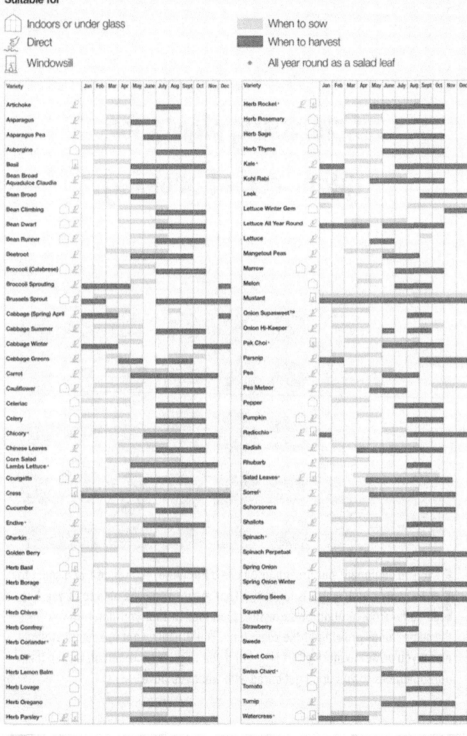

Indoors or under glass — When to sow

Direct — When to harvest

Windowsill — • All year round as a salad leaf

Variety	Jan Feb Mar Apr May June July Aug Sept Oct Nov Dec
Artichoke	
Asparagus	
Asparagus Pea	
Aubergine	
Basil	
Bean Broad Aquadulce Claudia	
Bean Broad	
Bean Climbing	
Bean Dwarf	
Bean Runner	
Beetroot	
Broccoli (Calabrese)	
Broccoli Sprouting	
Brussels Sprout	
Cabbage (Spring) April	
Cabbage Summer	
Cabbage Winter	
Cabbage Greens	
Carrot	
Cauliflower	
Celeriac	
Celery	
Chicory	
Chinese Leaves	
Corn Salad Lambs Lettuce	
Courgette	
Cress	
Cucumber	
Endive	
Gherkin	
Golden Berry	
Herb Basil	
Herb Borage	
Herb Chervil	
Herb Chives	
Herb Comfrey	
Herb Coriander	
Herb Dill	
Herb Lemon Balm	
Herb Lovage	
Herb Oregano	
Herb Parsley	

Variety	Jan Feb Mar Apr May June July Aug Sept Oct Nov Dec
Herb Rocket	
Herb Rosemary	
Herb Sage	
Herb Thyme	
Kale	
Kohl Rabi	
Leek	
Lettuce Winter Gem	
Lettuce All Year Round	
Lettuce	
Mangetout Peas	
Marrow	
Melon	
Mustard	
Onion Supasweet™	
Onion Hi-Keeper	
Pak Choi	
Parsnip	
Pea	
Pea Meteor	
Pepper	
Pumpkin	
Radicchio	
Radish	
Rhubarb	
Salad Leaves	
Sorrel	
Schorzonera	
Shallots	
Spinach	
Spinach Perpetual	
Spring Onion	
Spring Onion Winter	
Sprouting Seeds	
Squash	
Strawberry	
Swede	
Sweet Corn	
Swiss Chard	
Tomato	
Turnip	
Watercress	

- This handy guide will help you know what's in season for companion and succession planting -

You can keep in season with what would normally be growing at the time, or have melons in the dead of winter and butternut squash in the middle of summer. It's really up to you. Another fun thing to do is to cultivate some spring bulbs to give as gifts for occasions like Easter or Mother's Day. Planting some annuals to make flower arrangements with is also a lovely idea that will keep your gardening juices flowing and brighten your home or someone else's day. Don't forget that herb mixes and dried flowers also make terrific, thoughtful gifts!

Another way to maximize space is to companion plant your herbs and vegetables. That will keep things growing in every pot, even when veggies are done with their run and need to be replaced or succession planted. Because most herbs are perennials and most vegetables are annuals, those containers can pull double duty year-round. It can be tempting, though, to plant too many things in too small a space. Try to keep plants away from being directly on top of each other in a single container. A good rule is that if it seems like it's going to be too cramped, it probably is. Go with your guts, and always roam along the side of giving more space per plant, rather than less.

CHAPTER 13
Managing and operating a greenhouse

Let us understand some science behind growing the crops in different climatic conditions. Onwards, my fellow gardener!

Overwintering your Greenhouse

Let's get started with the cold part of the year. What you should be looking for is the availability of natural sunlight. As we had seen earlier, you should always seek to find places that provide you with enough sunlight. This is essential for growing crops, regardless of the climate you face (as winter typically provides less sunlight.) Another factor that you should take into consideration for winter specifically is the natural outdoor temperature.

Should you have a deficiency of both of the above factors (that is, proper sunlight and the right temperature), and then you can always make use of artificial lighting. Getting UV lamps is an effective way to do this. However, make sure you have the right UV scale. You do not want your plants to turn out deep fried!

But the above method is a last ditch effort. You see, the main purpose of having a greenhouse is to make use of natural light, heat, and temperature conditions for your plants.

To understand the ways in which you can make use of winter for your crops, it is important to get started with the science behind how plants make use of natural conditions.

You might be aware of the basics. Plants essentially convert carbon dioxide into oxygen. They also utilize water that they absorb through the roots and disperse through their leaves in a process called "transpiration." This water is the source of a number of nutrients for the plants. That is one reason why it is important to pay attention to this water consumption cycle of the plants when you have an artificial system for growing crops.

When there is an excess of humidity within the greenhouse, then it gets too dry for the plants. This prevents them from transpiring water fast enough. This adds stress to the plants, and they eventually begin to rot.

Different winter plants are used to different levels of humidity. However, when you typically consider plants that thrive during winter, then you are looking at those plants that receive the right temperature and the right levels of humidity. This means that while sunlight is necessary, it is the ability to control the flow of air, the temperature levels inside the greenhouse, and the water supply to the plants that matters.

Here are a few ways you can keep conditions during winter ideal for plant growth.

Temperature

This is an important factor for controlling humidity. What you should be ideally looking for is to utilize the low-level temperatures and find crops that grow in such conditions. Raising the temperature, while it may sound convenient, is rather counterintuitive, especially considering the electricity bill you might receive at the end of the month! However, if it is truly necessary, you can induce artificial lighting to grow certain plants. I would recommend you make use of the season rather than establishing alternatives in your greenhouse.

Airflow

Getting the right flow of air depends on ventilation. With the right air flow, you might be able to manage the humidity in your greenhouse. Make use of the vents in your greenhouse (if you have not considered adding vents to your greenhouse, then take this part as a note to do so) to induce a nice airflow. Adding exhaust fans to your greenhouse might also help you improve the conditions. An ideal way to go about constructing vents is to use this technique.

- Make sure that you place your exhaust fans near the edge of the ceiling.

- Then, place intake vents near the floor of the greenhouse.

This arrangement is useful to remove the damp interior air outside and allow in drier air. Why does dry air flow through the intake vents at the floor? That is simple; warm air rises and cold air settles down. Keeping the intake vents at the bottom give you access to this cold, dry air. By keeping the exhaust fan at the top, you are removing the warm air from the greenhouse. If you are wondering why we are removing the wet air from the greenhouse, then you should know that damp air is the reason for humidity. We are simply removing humidity by getting to the root of the problem.

Water

A very essential factor. Also, one that is quite overlooked, surprisingly. Water is useful to control the humidity of the greenhouse. I can probably imagine what some of you are thinking. Hold on! You just removed damp air, but you chose to keep water? What changed? Here is the thing. I am not talking about keeping water around. Rather, I am talking about supplying water to the plants. You see, despite the measures that we take to remove humidity, it always leaves an effect on your plants. Hence, ensure that you have a proper supply of water to your soil, giving the roots of the plants some much-needed nutrients.

With that, you are ready to grow crops during the winter.

Preparing your Greenhouse for spring

One of the things that you can do during spring (and practically any other time of the year) is adding compost to your soil.

This is a useful addition because it creates healthy and long-lasting soil. Additionally, it maintains the pH levels of the soil, gives the roots nutrients, and makes the soil ideal for planting. However, here is a tip I think would come in handy for you. Try to use cover crops, which are special crops that you can use to enrich and protect the soil. The way they work is that when you plant them, their roots dig into the soil and mixes up the essential nutrients. This is why, when you are in need of essential nutrients, you can simply plant these crops at the beginning of spring. By the time you harvest them, you will have soil rich in wonderful nutrients for your warm-season plants to enjoy.

You could also use certain quick cover crops that you can harvest in a short period of time. This allows you to grow the rest of your plants in the same season. First, check the weather and make sure that the temperature is not extreme. Then go ahead and plant these cover crops. A few examples of these crops are oats, barley, and mustard. These crops provide you with essential organic materials for the vegetables and plants that you would like to grow later. A popular crop for cover has been ryegrass, but it is known to return during the summer as a stubborn weed (removing it is a cumbersome process). Your next alternative would be to use mustard, but make sure you get yourself high quality plants. Mustard is known to harbor diseases that can harm other plants, though humans are safe from this.

CHAPTER 14
Potential Greenhouse Problems

We have tackled so much information together in this book so far. We have already covered everything that you need to know about building a greenhouse, growing plants in your greenhouse, and finding success in doing so. We've talked about all the different ways of planting and all the different tips and tricks that we have for you. Now that we've reached the end, let's look back and talk about some common greenhouse problems that you might face. Issues can pop up in greenhouses no matter how well you treat your plants. Do you not feel bad if any of these problems pop up? Simply look back at this information and figure out how you can solve the issue quickly and effectively. We are going to go over every common greenhouse problem that you might come up against you in your journey of growing a garden inside of a greenhouse. We will look into the problem in detail, who learn why it occurs, and learn how to fix it. Let's get started.

First, let's look into what to do if you get bugs in your greenhouse. Is there something that you would think of dealing with outside? Obviously, you do not want to need to deal with them inside of your greenhouse. The first reason is that you are already in a structure—you should not have to deal with something like bugs. The second reason is if bugs are in your greenhouse, it is not like they're merely going to be like when they are outside. If bugs are in your greenhouse, they probably think that they are there to stay. You will need to do something to get them out of your greenhouse. They are not going to fly away like they were outside.

Let's start by looking into why bugs get into greenhouses. If there is any space that allows insects to get into your greenhouse—like a crack or hole or even vent or door that was open for a few seconds—bugs can get in. Bugs go inside greenhouses because they know they're filled with plants and because they want to pollinate them. Bugs can also go to clean houses to explore. Other bugs are looking for plants to eat. You really do not want these latter bugs in your greenhouse. You definitely do not want your plants to get eaten by anyone except for you.

Next, let's look into some ways that you can prevent bugs from getting into your greenhouse. One of the easiest ways to avoid getting bumped into your greenhouses is to look at the things that you bring inside. If you are bringing inside a plant, make sure there are no bugs in it. If you are bringing in new soil, make sure you do the same. Anything that you bring in should be checked to ensure that there are no bugs that could hurt your plants on them.

Another thing that you can do to avoid getting bugs in your greenhouses to make sure that they do not have a way in. Make sure that all cracks and holes are filled. Also, if you have a fence, you could consider putting a screen on them. You can put screens on the windows as well. You can also make sure that when you come in and out of the greenhouse, you do so quickly, and you do not leave the door open.

It is also a good idea not to plant anything around the outside of your greenhouse. If you put plants around the outside of your greenhouse, these plants can attract bugs. If you attract insects next to your greenhouse, they will likely know that there are plants inside, and they will probably find a way in. You want to keep all of your outdoor plants far away from the greenhouse to avoid this happening.

Now, let's look into what to do if you already have bugs inside of your greenhouse. In an outdoor garden, you might reach for the pesticides. This is not a great idea inside of a greenhouse not only because they are toxic chemicals, but because in such a small space, they can be a hazard. One helpful way to catch bugs inside of your greenhouse is to use bug traps like tape. You can hang out tape all-around in your greenhouse, and it will not affect your plants. It will, however, catch the bugs that you do not want to be there. You could also consider making sure to get rid of anything that will attract bugs. For example, make sure that there is no standing water available in your greenhouse. If your bugs are not attracted to anything inside of your greenhouse, they may leave. If you are really having a hard time with bugs in your greenhouse, you could always ask a professional exterminator for help.

Something that can be problematic is your greenhouse's diseases. Many different things can cause diseases in your plants. These problems can come from mold, bacteria, and viruses. Greenhouse diseases, sometimes, can be hard to beat. Let's look into some ways that you can prevent these diseases from occurring in your greenhouse.

What is the most important thing that you can do to prevent disease in your greenhouses? It is to sanitize. You want to make sure that you sanitize everything after you use it. You will need to sanitize 2, trays, and even shelves. If you do not sanitize your tools, it increases your risk of spreading disease inside of your greenhouse from plant to plant. This is because if one plant had a disease and you used a shovel to scoop it out and throw it away, and then use the same shovel in another plant, the new plant would probably get the disease as well just from being touched with the same shovel. The spread of disease in plants inside of greenhouses is really similar to the spread of disease in humans. If you stay clean, you will have a much better chance of not spreading diseases.

You allow someone to watch your humidity and make sure that you are greenhouse does not get overly humid. If your greenhouse is too humid, mold and fungus are likely to grow on your soil. If these grow in your soil, your plants will get the disease because of them. Mold and fungus can also spread very quickly and easily. It is something that you really want to avoid having in your greenhouse.

When watering your plants, you will want to make sure that the tool does not touch your plant's insurgencies, and you will also want to make sure that the water does not splash while you are watering. If water splashes from one plant to another, it can spread disease. Because of this, you will want to use a tool for watering that does not allow water to splash. You will want to use the tool that has a light spray that soaks into the soil and does not splash at all.

One last thing that you can do to protect your plants from disease is to look at them every day. Walk around your greenhouse and look for signs of disease. Look for things that seem out of the ordinary. If you see a plant that does not look healthy, consider taking it out of the greenhouse and quarantining it for a while. This will allow you to tell if the plant is infected with the disease as well as keep it away from other healthy plants to make sure that they do not catch a disease if it has one. With this process, it is helpful to know what plants look like when they are diseased. If the plant has mold or fungus, you will probably be able to tell right away. If it has mold growing in the soil or mushrooms growing in the ground, it means that it has mold or fungus. This is one of the most natural diseases to tell if your plant has. Another sign that your plant has a disease is that it has large, raised brown lumps on its leaves. These lumps typically mean the plant is sick. Plants that seem to be dying even though you are taking great care of them can be diseased as well. Any plant that is showing signs that are not normal should be taken away from your healthy plants just in case a disease is present.

Next, let's look into what to do if a plant is severely diseased. If you see that, make sure you take it out of the greenhouse right away. This will help to make it not infect other pants. Also, you should look at helping it right away—especially if you are able to save your plant when all signs of the disease are gone and bring it back to the greenhouse. If not, at least, you only lost one plant and not your entire greenhouse to a disease.

Diseases in greenhouses are not fun to deal with. You should be able to handle them with success. If you take the necessary precautions to make sure that diseases do not enter your plants and take it seriously when a plant is looking unhealthy, you should have success in keeping this problem away.

CHAPTER 15
Pollination in a Greenhouse

Birds, bees and butterflies are also the pollinators of nature. The same shield shielding plants from adverse growth conditions will also discourage the pollinators from doing their work. And how does pollination work inside the enclosed structure? Also in safe greenhouses, a minor intrusion will ensure plants can be successfully pollinated.

Manual Polishing: It can take some time but softly touching flowers may unleash pollen. Disturbing male to female flowers disperse pollen with each bloom.

Device Pollination: When manual pollination cannot work into your timetable, you can use battery-operated pollinating devices. As an operator it still needs you so these resources speed the mission.

Bee Pollinated: By nature bees are great pollinators. For pollination purposes certain bumble bee pollinators may be born. You can buy a box or a bee hive and put it in your greenhouse, as long as you do supply these pollinators with the supplementary food source.

Using fans to dry plants before pollinating them in an extremely humid climate. High level of humidity can cause pollen to bind together in clumps causing ineffective pollination attempts. Pollinating plants from 10 a.m.-3 p.m. is also possible.

Greenhouse Business

Start a greenhouse company by following these steps: the ideal business plan has been discovered and you are now able to take the next step. Starting a company is more than just registering it with the Department. We've put together this quick guide to start your company in greenhouse. Such moves will ensure the new company is well developed, correctly licensed and consistent with the law.

Phase 1: Plan your company a simple plan is key to entrepreneurial success. It will help you chart your company information and uncover a few unknowns. Two relevant things to remember are: • what are the start-up costs and the continuing costs?

- Who the target audience is?

- How long would it take for you to even break?

- What company are you going to name?

Fortunately we did a lot of the work for you.

How much would it cost to start a greenhouse business?

Money will be spent on the greenhouse building or leasing, as well as on production, drainage, manure, fans and hoses, benches and chairs, cash registers, insurance and wages for employees.

What are the current Greenhouse Sector expenses?

You may purchase greenhouse space, or rent an existing plant. The room would possibly cost a considerable amount of money. Expect paying up a few hundred thousand dollars to buy the amount of land available for an enormous greenhouse. If you rent such a space, it would undoubtedly cost several thousand dollars a month, precisely because the inventory requires an excess of space to produce and present.

You'll need to buy all kinds of trees, flowers, fruit, seeds and other gardening and landscaping products. Expect investing $5,000-$10,000 or more on the initial inventory, with at least $500-$1,000 on recurring inventory costs per month. The precise number for your greenhouse depends on the scale.

Services like water and power are estimated to cost several hundred dollars a month. Budget the publicity costs of at least a few hundred dollars a month. Employees would need compensation of at least $10 an hour, which in certain cases will definitely be higher. When you finally recruit communications and accounting experts they are expected to demand $35,000-$50,000 annual wages.

What will be the target market?

A company owner who wants a diverse selection of flowers and plants is the perfect client. Examples include farmers, owners of kindergartens, grocers, florists etc. Greenhouse company owners often tend to market green-thumbs to homeowners. The objective is to sell a wide variety of products to each client and ensure a steady supply of flowers, trees, produce and other vegetables in order to keep supplies as fresh as possible.

Why does a greenhouse company make money?

Greenhouse companies make money from the sale to buyers of trees, flowers, produce and other gardening and landscaping products.

So much does it cost you customers?

Greenhouse goods prices differ according to plant quality, desirability, lifetime and a variety of other factors. It is possible to sell seeds, bulbs, and vegetables for sums ranging from a few dollars to $100 and more. Seeds usually cost between 75 cents per packet and several dollars. Supplies for planting and landscaping usually range from $5 to $50

How much benefit will a greenhouse enterprise make?

In its initial years a greenhouse will make a tidy profit, particularly if it is situated in an area where people are passionate about gardening, greenery and nature. A greenhouse is not out of the question making an income of $50,000-$100,000 a year. Profits will hit several hundred thousand dollars or more a year if the greenhouse owner extends operations and opens new locations.

How do you sell your company more?

A greenhouse owner can sell gardening and landscaping related products such as hand trowels, sprinklers, gardening gloves, hoes, shovels, shears, loppers, pitchforks, tillers, plants, soil, mulch, peat moss, etc. Selling vegetable and/or flower seeds may produce additional income. Any owners of a greenhouse earn extra money by paying for deliveries.

What are you going to call your business?

It's incredibly necessary to pick the correct name. It is best to verify if the company name you chose is eligible as a web domain and to lock it early enough that no one else will claim it.

Move 2: Creating a legal corporation such as an LLC protects you from being legally accountable if your greenhouse company is being sued. There are several corporate models to pick from that include: Corporations, LLCs, and DBA's.

Stage 3: Tax registration you'll need to apply for a number of federal and state taxes before you can open for service.

You would need to apply for an EIN to file for the taxes. It is completely free and simple!

Phase 4: Open a business bank account & credit card the use of dedicated business banking and credit cards is essential to the security of personal properties.

If your personal and company liabilities are combined, in case your company is sued your financial properties (your house, vehicle, and other valuables) are at risk. This is referred to in company law as breaking the corporate veil.

Open a business bank account • It divides your financial funds from the funds of the organization which are required for the security of corporate assets.

• It simplifies budgets and tax reporting, too.

Use a corporate credit card • this helps distinguish personal and company spending by placing all of the costs of the corporate in one location.

• This also creates the financial history of the business and can be valuable for later raising capital and investment.

STEP 5: develop tax accounting reporting your different costs and revenue streams is essential to knowing your tax 'financial results. Additionally, keeping correct and comprehensive accounts significantly simplifies the yearly tax return.

STEP 6: Obtain required permits and licenses Failure to obtain required permits and licenses will result in heavy fines or even closure of your company.

State & Local Business Licensing Regulations The operation of a greenhouse company may require state permits and licenses. Learn more about licensing conditions in your state by visiting SBA's State Licensing and Permit Guide.

Occupancy certificate Companies operate from a physical venue, such as a greenhouse, usually need an Occupancy Certificate (CO). A CO maintains compliance with all of the building codes, zoning rules, and municipal legislation.

- If you intend to rent a greenhouse: o It is usually the duty of the owner to acquire a CO. o. Confirm, before contracting, that the owner has or may procure a legitimate CO specific to a greenhouse company.

- A new CO is always to be released following a big upgrade. When your place of business is refurbished before opening, it is advised that you have wording in the lease agreement specifying that lease payments do not start before a new CO is released.

- If you intend to buy or build a greenhouse: o you must be liable for receiving a legitimate CO from the local authorities.

- Check all building codes and zoning standards for the area of your business and ensure that your greenhouse company is in practice and capable of securing a CO. STEP 7: Get liability insurance is highly recommended by all business owners. If you hire staff, insurance for workers 'compensation can be a legal obligation in your Jurisdiction.

Phase 8: Identifying your brand your brand is what your company stands for, and how the market perceives your business. A good name will help the company differentiate itself from rivals.

How to encourage and sell a greenhouse business Advertise your greenhouse business in a range of ways, from local newspapers to radio ads, banners, local TV advertisements and more. Creating an informative website that highlights your vast inventory would also help. Invest in a program to enhance search engine optimization (SEO) and boost access to the website, blog and social media channels.

It is important that you create your greenhouse as a reputable brand worthy of trust and loyalty to the customers. Please give your initial customers and they will spread the greenhouse message to friends, families and colleagues. This is the best marketing form: Totally free and highly effective.

How to keep consumers coming back the only way to draw and maintain consumers within the company is to build a sterling reputation. If your product is top-notch, the rates will be affordable, and the employees will be friendly, local residents will come in droves. Your plants and flowers are imperative to stand the test of time. When they die in the days after delivery, consumers spread the message around the world that the goods are of poor quality and not worth buying.

Phase 9: Build an Online Presence a company website offers consumers with an ability to know more about an industry and the goods or services you provide. You may also use the social media to draw new buyers or companies.

CHAPTER 16
Portable Greenhouses

A full-size greenhouse is wonderful, but not everyone has the space or money for one. If you don't, then there are alternatives that will give you many of the benefits without the expense.

The above picture shows you my portable greenhouse which I bought reduced at the end of the growing season. It has given me a few years' service and is ideal for starting off seeds close to my back door, so they are easy to tend.

Portable greenhouses are much smaller and more fragile, but if you don't have enough space for a full-size greenhouse, then these are worth getting. You may only be able to get a few tomatos and pepper plants in it, but it is more than you would otherwise have been able to grow!

Yes, I've squeezed rather a lot into that small greenhouse, but I got a decent crop. Plants were taken out during the day and warm weather and then put back in overnight to minimize the risk of disease and help air circulation. I got a great crop!

One advantage of these smaller greenhouses is that they allow you to, at the very least, start your seeds off early and protect them from unexpected frosts.

Portable plastic greenhouses come in all shapes and sizes suitable for a wide range of budgets. As these tend to come in large boxes, they are usually heavily discounted at the end of the growing season because the retailer doesn't want to take up precious storage space which could be used for more lucrative Christmas stock. Perfect for you to buy for the following year!

When I had a small concrete yard rather than a garden I bought a 4-foot wide and 3-foot deep portable, plastic greenhouse that stood about 7 feet tall. As there was no soil, this was all I had to grow in, so it got filled with tomato and pepper plants which grew remarkably well. Eventually, I was assigned an allotment to grow vegetables on, and then I kept the plastic greenhouse at home to start my seeds off. New seeds need a lot of attention, so it was much easier to have them close to hand rather than having to drive to my allotment.

These greenhouses come in a huge variety of shapes and sizes, so you will be able to find something suitable for the space you have in mind for it. Even if you have a greenhouse and a garden they can be useful as extra space or to start seeds off nearer to your door.

One word of caution though, these are much more fragile than traditional greenhouses and will need securing to the ground. I put grow bags on the bottom metal poles to provide weight so that it couldn't blow away. You should also use guy ropes if possible and position your portable greenhouse in a sheltered location.

Like normal greenhouses, these will get very hot and suffer from many of the same problems with overcrowding and poor air circulation. I would recommend that on warmer days you leave the door open.

The plastic covers can tear, but replacements are available, often from the original store you bought your portable greenhouse from or online.

A low to the ground, portable greenhouse can be used as a cold frame. These are great to have as well as a normal greenhouse because you can use them to help harden off your seedlings before planting them out.

Some people will recommend you avoid these plastic greenhouses as they only last a season but, in my experience, if they are looked after properly and located well they will last several years. The one I am currently growing in has been in use for three years and has still got a couple of years of service left in it.

The more expensive plastic greenhouses tend to have thicker plastic covers. These heavy duty covers will last a few more years as they are harder to damage. When exposed to UV light plastic has a tendency to become brittle and break, but if you buy a cover with UV protection, and then it will last a little longer.

I would recommend that you take the portable greenhouse down when winter approaches. Snow, frost and high winds can damage the greenhouse and shorten its lifespan. As these greenhouses can be put up in 10 to 20 minutes, this isn't a great hardship.

Cold Frames

Cold frames are a very useful accompaniment to a greenhouse. At one time these were found in every garden attached to the greenhouse but now have become free standing structures. These are used as mini greenhouses to start off seeds and harden off plants. Although they have declined in popularity somewhat due to the cheap availability of glass greenhouses they are still handy to have in your garden.

The cold frame provides a sheltered, warm environment where you can germinate seeds and start your seedlings off. As it is sheltered, a cold frame is ideal for growing plants such as cucumbers. These tend to be fairly low to the ground, so they aren't suitable for larger plants such as tomatoes.

For hardening off your plants, a cold frame is ideal. You move the plant to the cold frame, leaving the lid open for longer and longer until the plants get acclimatized to the weather.

Cold frames come in all shapes and sizes, and as the gardener often builds them, they are often unique in their design. You can purchase cold frames online and from gardening stores where they can cost anything from tens of dollars upwards.

Of course, if you don't want to buy one you can make your own cold frame, which many people do. You can recycle old windows, bricks, and wood to make a cold frame that fits the space you have in mind for it.

The traditional cold frame was a brick-walled cold frame, usually attached to the sunny side of the greenhouse (which would have been several layers of brick with the greenhouse on top). These would have varied in size with some being tall enough to stand in.

Larger brick cold frames were used as hotbeds, filled with rotting manure so the heat would warm the plants inside.

These are still popular with gardeners because they are easy to build from reclaimed bricks but nowadays tend to be free standing.

A wooden sided cold frame is very easy to build and can either be a wooden frame with glass in or solid wooden sides. Almost anyone will be able to build one of these, and if you have solid wooden sides, then this will help retain warmth, particularly if you insulate the wood with bubble wrap or something similar.

You can buy wooden sided cold frames though like wooden greenhouses they tend to be a little bit more expensive.

A cheaper option if you are buying a cold frame is one made of aluminum and glass. The glass sides let more light in which helps prevent the plants from becoming too leggy. However, the downside is that they do not retain heat, as well as a wooden or brick, sided cold frame. Also being glass, you have the same set of problems as you do with a glass greenhouse.

You can buy plastic cold frames which are twin walled, so they retain heat better. While they do not let in as much light, they protect your plants better from the cold.

One thing to be careful of with a wooden framed cold frame is that the wood can warp in hot, cold and wet weather. Make sure you treat the wood every year to protect it.

If you use raised beds, then these are very easy for you to convert to a cold frame. You can build a roof over the top of it. However, you need to be careful to ensure there is sufficient air circulation as it the seal is too good then it will encourage fungal growth.

There are plenty of woodworking plans available online for making your own cold frame, but at the end of the day, you can make something that suits your needs and the space you have for it. Your cold frame needs to be located somewhere that gets plenty of sunlight, particularly during the spring months. It needs to be easy to open and of a sufficient size for what you want to put in it.

Pit Greenhouses Explained

A pit greenhouse, or underground greenhouse, is a subject all of its one, one that could have an entire book written about it. It is an interesting variation on the greenhouse and is very useful in colder areas with heavy ground frosts.

For people who live in colder areas, a pit greenhouse will extend the growing season significantly and help you grow plants that you would otherwise be unable to grow due to the cold weather.

These are popular in the mountains of South America, Tibet, Japan, Mongolia as well as the Northern United States and Canada.

Pit greenhouses are sometimes referred to as walipini and use the heat of the sun and the insulation of the surrounding earth to warm the area you grow in. They are simple to build, cheap and very effective.

Typically, you will build a bit greenhouse into a natural slope, so very little of it is exposed to the cold. They are usually built of clay, stone or brick and are between 6 and 8 feet deep.

Usually, these are walk-in structures, and they can be heated if you prefer with electric or paraffin heaters. Without heating, they can keep the temperature a good 20F warmer than outside.

You will position your pit greenhouse, so it is south facing to maximize the amount of sun it gets, particularly on shorter days. The roof is commonly angled to let in as much light as possible.

When building a pit greenhouse, you need to ensure it is above the water table. If not, then you are going to find your greenhouse regularly flooded. You need the bottom of your pit greenhouse to be at least five feet above the water table.

The pit is marked out and dug, then lined with insulating material and construction material, e.g. brick. You may, depending on how cold it is where you live, build a double wall with insulating material in between the layers of brick.

One construction material that is used is bags of earth. These are the bags used in sandbags but filled with the earth excavated from the pit. These can be used internally as insulation and to build up the second wall.

The roof is then built up, so it is slanted at an angle. Again, good quality material is best to ensure it provides sufficient insulation. If you can build in some windows that open, then you will be able to provide ventilation in the summer months. As you know, this is vital to prevent fungal infections and other problems.

In extremely cold weather, the roof can be covered with further insulating material to prevent heat loss.

If your area suffers from heavy snowfall then you need to ensure that the roof angle is sufficient to prevent snow settling on the roof. The weight of the snow could end up damaging or even breaking your roof.

CHAPTER 17

Cleaning your Greenhouses

Like our houses, the greenhouses require daily maintenance to keep them in good shape and to maintain the required standards of cleanliness and hygiene. This comes down to looking after the layout of the greenhouse – within and outside – its heating, ventilation and irrigation systems, and maybe most importantly, the growing ecosystem itself.

General Maintenance

The greenhouse should be checked regularly for any broken or cracked glass, particularly after high winds, and the panels should be replaced as required. The frame, too, needs to be inspected routinely to make sure it is in good order. Although aluminum enclosures are usually reasonably low-maintenance, wooden enclosures will need to be regularly painted or treated with an acceptable preservative – making sure that none of them touches the plants, of course – and any rotting areas will need to be repaired.

Cleaning

Regular cleaning helps to maintain the structure of the greenhouse and dirty windows reduces the level of light – which can lead to problems with propagation, such as tight seedlings. The best times to have a big clean-up are in the spring – just before you start sowing – or in the early autumn before half-hardy plants are brought in for the winter.

Cleaning the exterior of the greenhouse is best achieved on a relatively breezy day, using warm water and a sponge, allowing the wind to dry the glass and stop leaving too much in the way of streaks. Aluminum framed greenhouses can be particularly prone to the collection of grime beneath the joints between the panels – the jet-wash attachment for the hose or the gentle scraping with the old plant label often shifts the dirt very successfully.

Regular, thorough cleaning of the interior of the greenhouse is essential, not only to create a pleasant environment in which to work but also as a significant part of the control of pests and diseases. It has also been said that it will be difficult to overemphasize the value of cleanliness for greenhouse management – so doing a good job here will save hours of trouble!

When beginning, make sure that the electricity is switched off, that the heaters and other electrical appliances are unplugged and that the sockets are sealed. If the temperature outside is too cold, remove all plants, containers, pots and staging – protecting any tender or semi-hard plants with horticultural fleece or putting them inside a shed or garage while you're working. This is the perfect time to scrutinize each plant, to remove any sick or damaged leaves and to discard anything dead or dying.

Greenhouse Weed Control

All spent compost or growing bags should be disposed of, and the floor swept away to avoid fallen leaves and general trash, and then any beds weeded. Now that the greenhouse has been emptied, the glass, the pathways and any brickwork should be thoroughly cleaned with warm water and an appropriate disinfectant, allowing them to dry thoroughly before returning the evicted plants to their proper places.

Check the Equipment

The heating, ventilation and irrigation systems are essential to the greenhouse, and they should not be forgotten or ignored. Daily checks – and, where necessary, servicing – of these main items are crucial, whether you do so yourself or call outside support. At the same time, pots, containers, seating, spread tables, capillary mats and the like should also be routinely sterilized to popular the risk of pests and disease and any lighting systems inspected.

Maintaining the Growing Environment

The dry, humid atmosphere of the greenhouse is suitable for many pests and diseases that can spread depressively quickly when given the opportunity, but keeping the greenhouse clean and tidy will significantly reduce the risk that they will become a problem. Supporting those plants that need it – and tying them in their developing shoots – combined with a regime of pruning, picking, potting and pinching plants as required and a thorough weeding around the beds would help.

Providing some form of shade as necessary can also be of great benefit – preventing leaves that are scorched and the almost unavoidable resulting disease attacks that the weakened and damaged plant would experience. It is necessary to remember that the perfect growing conditions for plants provided by the greenhouse are just as tailor-made for any number of bacteria, fungi and other unwanted guests. Part of daily greenhouse maintenance also includes being always on the lookout for pests and diseases – such as aphids, red spider mites, mealy bugs, mildew and botrytis – and ready to handle them promptly.

Spring cleaning is just as crucial to our greenhouses as our homes. Still, in addition to a one-off annual cleaning, routine maintenance is essential to keep everything running smoothly. However, with a bit of attention to one or two key elements, keeping our greenhouses at its peak does not need to pose too much of a problem or take too much of our time.

As the summer slips gently into the autumn, and the days begin to get shorter and noticeably colder, there are a few jobs that need to be done around the greenhouse to get things ready for the coming winter.

Seasonal Maintenance

Autumn is a good time for a little routine maintenance of the greenhouse – cleaning and repairing the structure inside and outside, thoroughly disinfecting the staging and equipment and ensuring that the heating system is in good order before the temperature drops. This can be done as early as late August or the first week of September, especially if you have a lot of tender plants to protect – British weather being what it is, you can never be sure when the first frost comes, so it's just as good to be prepared!

It is a great idea to use this opportunity to clean and inspect gutters for leaks, either by replacing or repairing, as appropriate — leaky gutting can often cause wood to rot in wood-framed greenhouses and does little to improve aluminum ones either. It is worth keeping a close eye on gutters and downspouts through the autumn, particularly if there are trees in the area, as they can block leaves very quickly at this time of year.

As the autumn progresses and the light levels drop, any shades put up during the summer to protect the delicate leaves from scorching should now be removed. If your greenhouse is on the exposed site or you keep the plants particularly tender, it may be time to think about insulation.

Plant Care

Before nights turn too cold, young or frost-sensitive plants need to be brought in, and it is an excellent plan to check them at this point for any signs of pests and diseases to avoid any problems in the greenhouse. With the greenhouse now often at its most crowded, careful attention needs to be paid to the first signs of any ill-health — mildews and molds being a particular potential nuisance at this point in the gardener's calendar.

As the indoor temperature becomes cooler, it is critical that all watering is done carefully to avoid making perfect conditions for the grey mold (Botrytis) that attacks a wide range of plants and thrives in a cold, damp climate, thus aiming for a slightly dry atmosphere. Prompt treatment will also help, but any plant that has gone too far will — sadly — have to be discarded and burned to prevent the spread of the disease.

Even though the summer has just passed, autumn is a good time to think about getting ready for the next growing season. A wide variety of different plants can be propagated from cuttings and overwintered in the greenhouse to give them the start of the New Year, including several tender flowering plants, shrubs, spices, carnations, fuchsias and pelargoniums.

Sown in early September, annuals can also be grown in the greenhouse — provided they get enough light — to provide a very colorful early show in the spring. Again, there is no shortage of suitable candidates, including calendulas, carnations, cornflowers, nemesis, godets, phlox and schizanthus. Early vegetables can also be sown, and bulbs can be planted in October to offer a welcome splash of color as the winter draws to a close.

There's always something a little sad about putting the garden to bed as autumn gradually starts to give way to winter – but at least the greenhouse not only allows you to shield your choice of tender plants from the worst of the cold but also to get ahead of the game for the coming season. With all your autumn maintenance and cleaning done, you will have just about enough time to pour through all those seed catalogues before you need to start sowing!

CHAPTER 18

Controlling greenhouse pests and diseases

A greenhouse is an excellent tool for keen gardeners. It offers a much-needed space for growing plants outside of the usual summer season. However, while sheltering your plants from the components, a greenhouse can also be prone to harboring diseases and pests that could wreck all your hard labor. Hence the need to be more proactive in giving your greenhouse plants the best possible protection. The following are the ways to protect your plants.

Maintain a Clean Greenhouse

To prevent any kind of pest or disease, cleanliness is the priority. As part of your general maintenance, the ideal thing is to thoroughly empty and clean out your greenhouse once every year. It has to do with washing down the surfaces and windows, cleaning all the pots and hosing off the floors. Removing plant debris, weeding in and outside of the greenhouse, and reducing algae are also part of the greenhouse sanitation. By doing all these, you will have a fresh, bug-free start for growing each year.

Examine Your Plants

It is crucial to inspect all your plants before bringing them to the greenhouse to avoid spreading of bugs inside. Just as crops and flowers like the warmness of a greenhouse so do pests and they increase rapidly in the heat. Therefore, ensure to thoroughly scrutinize any new plants for signs of larvae or insects on the stem or leaves before taking them in.

Sterilize Your Tools

A good number of gardeners will often use the same tools all around the garden, moving them around the lawn, compost heap, vegetable patch, flower beds, shed, and greenhouse. This implies that they can easily pick up bugs from the soil outdoors and infect the plants inside the building. So to be very cautious, you will want to give your trowels, spades, and other equipment a good clean after every use. Soaking them in soapy water will do well.

Eliminate Every Source of Standing Water

Standing water is favorable to the increase of pests and diseases so ensure there is no source of stagnant water around and inside the greenhouse. Be it puddle or jug; get rid of every single source of water.

Isolate Your New Plants

Your greenhouse might be free from pests, but new plants can turn out to be buggy. As soon as possible, the new plants can infest your whole greenhouse with pests. To avoid this scenario, you may need to put your new plants in an isolation chamber until you confirm they're pest free. You may make use of an aquarium with tight-fitting cover if you do not have an isolation chamber.

Use Insect Barriers and Traps

There is possibility that bugs will always make a way into your greenhouse. Use a simple greenhouse pests control products to catch them where they fly. Products such as wasp traps and hanging fly papers, you can also use spider spray at the entrance.

Use netting

Greenhouses require proper aeration, and it is not ideal to seal them up absolutely to prevent pests from entering. But you could reduce the number of big flying insects that come in by hanging netting, open windows, or other vent points.

Move pots outside in the heat

In the summer periods, a greenhouse will usually become hot and dry through the day. Taking plants in pots outside will not only help in cooling down the plants but also cut down the buildup of spider mites on them. Spider mites multiply in numbers in warm climates, so the ideal thing is to keep the greenhouse aerated and also use a mister to keep the humidity up. If you are leaving the house for the day, it's ideal to douse the floor of your greenhouse with water, which would evaporate into the air through the rest of the day.

Use potting soil

Often ordinary garden soil will be packed with a lot of insect eggs, creepy crawlies and other pests. Therefore, for the plants inside containers in the greenhouse, its best to use a good potting soil or compost for potting them. The soil should be rich in nutrients, sterilized free from any diseases and pests to help the plants grow.

Practice crop rotation

If you plant directly into the ground in your greenhouses, obviously you will not have much better control over the spread of pests and diseases inside the soil. Crop rotation is a better way to combat this by growing different type of plant in the structure each year. It will discourage the building up of pests in the soil since the same plant usually promotes similar kinds of pests.

Freeze the pests

This is an extreme measure which you can practice annually if you think your greenhouse is overwhelmed. In the winter period, open up all the windows and doors for one or two days to enable your greenhouse to reach a chilling point. Doing so the temperature will drop drastically, and any pests inside including their larvae and eggs will be destroyed. The plants will survive this as long as it is not chill for too long.

Use biological pest control

You can combat many common greenhouse pests such as spider mites, whitefly, and vine weevil grubs using biological control method. Every pest has their corresponding organism which you can purchase and bring in to area infested to feed on the bugs; this will put their population under control. When the pests are wiped out, the control organisms die out since no other food source for them, so do not be troubled about them damaging your plants.

Use a Pest Control Agency

In spite of your best efforts, you still notice the persistence of pests in your greenhouse. Hire a commercial pest control agency that employs an integrated management approach to pest-proof your greenhouse. These agencies are equipped with the know-how to manage greenhouse pests. They do everything from moisture control to rodent control, inspection, and sanitation. They have all the techniques and tools required to quickly identify and successfully get rid of pests and bugs from your greenhouse.

CHAPTER 19

Temperature and light requirements for your plant

The amount of light inside the greenhouse determines the level of sunlight in the greenhouse. If the amount of sunlight in the greenhouse is not strong enough, you can supplement it with artificial light.

Before choosing the lighting system to use for boosting plant growth, you need to determine the amount of solar radiation available in that area, as that will affect the amount of light needed for photosynthesis.

Others factors you need to look at are the size and type of greenhouse structure. You also need to consider the crops growing, as some of them require high-intensity light, while others will do better in low light or shade.

You should consider the space available for hanging the lighting system, and it should be easy to adjust based on the crops' needs. For example, as some plants, like fruits, increase in height as they grow, the lighting system should be moved upwards. Therefore, you need to factor in the wiring system and the socket space.

Some of the tools for providing artificial light include:

Light intensity meter: This instrument has an installed universal-sensor probe that measures the intensity of light at any angle. The equipment monitor can maintain an ideal growing light for all plants in the garden.

Grow lights: Grow lights are excellent for providing a cool and warm light for the growth of house plants, herbs, and fruits. The grow lights act as a replacement of sunlight when growing plants indoors. There are different types of grow lights in the market to choose from, such as fluorescent, LEDs, high pressure sodium, among others.

Seedling lights: As the seeds germinate, they require a lot of light; therefore, you need to place them in an area where they can have a maximum access to light. Each plant grown requires a different light intensity, and most plants in a greenhouse garden require a high light intensity to flourish. You can have fluorescent bulbs installed in the garden to provide maximum light to all your crops.

High Intensity Discharge lamp (HID): If you have a large greenhouse structure with big plants like fruits and flowers, you need to install HID lamps. These lamps emit more light compared to other types of lights, boosting plant growth. The lamp fixtures have reflectors fitted on it to reflect the light back to the crops.

This type of lamp produces a lot of heat, so you should keep it far away from the plants to avoid burning their leaves.

LED Lights: LED lights are suitable for vegetables and herbs. They're the best greenhouse lights and the most efficient for quick plant growth. The lights are long-lasting and easy to install.

Temperature Control and Heating System Equipment

To control the temperature, you need to install an electronic controller in the garden. This control will monitor and manage the temperatures of the heating system and ventilation equipment.

Thermostats: If you have a small greenhouse garden, you can use thermostats that record accurate temperatures within the garden, and they automatically control the temperature in a specific area. Make sure it is installed based on the plant height as this will make it easy to capture accurate readings on temperature conditions.

Thermometer: A thermometer measures the maximum and minimum temperature inside the garden and monitors any temperature changes. It helps in maintaining perfect temperatures for the growth of plants.

When buying thermometer for the greenhouse, look for one that is reset by a magnet. Although there are other types, the one with a magnet is highly recommended for greenhouses.

Hot air furnace or unit heaters: The unit heater is suitable when the greenhouse is shutdown during the winter season to drain water system. Installing unit heaters is one of the best decisions you can make for your crop production, as they control the temperature inside the greenhouse.

There are different types of heaters and based on your garden needs, such as gas, electric, or propane. You can also choose to use vented on non-vented heaters.

EPDM tubing: Temperature control on the benches or floor is also important. You can place the EPDM tubing on the concrete floor or in a sand layer to provide floor heating. If you plant your crops on the benches, you can place the EPDM tubing on the bench or use a low output radiation pin, which you would place under the bench to keep the area warm.

Hot water boiler: A hot water boiler is the best for maintaining the heating system. Make sure the water temperatures don't go beyond 75°F (24°C). The root zone heat provides the uniform temperatures of 70°F to 75°F (21°C to 24°C), which is essential for all plant growth. Root zone heat provides 25% of the heat needed for the coldest nights, while the remaining 75% heat comes from heat exchangers or a radiation pin installed under the gutters or around the perimeter of the greenhouse.

Humidistat: Humidistat equipment is needed to control moisture or humidity within the greenhouse.

In a large-scale operation, you can easily integrate computer controls in the ventilation, lighting, and heating systems. Using computer-controlled systems ensures automatic control of environmental conditions within the greenhouse.

Ventilation Equipment

A proper ventilation system contributes to the growth of your plants. Sunlight changes throughout the year can cause temperature changes in the garden, so you need to have a good venting system installed to control the temperatures.

Vents: You can install vents on the roof or on the sides of the structure. Rooftop vents are the most common and one of the best venting systems.

If you're not around throughout the day, an automatic venting system will be ideal for you.

Exhaust fans: You would use exhaust fans to whisk away excess air and ensure there is a constant supply of fresh air inside.

Water Management Equipment Irrigation Equipment

If you're using plug trays with small cells for growing the crops, then you should have a programmed computer irrigation system to water different section of crops at different rates. Automating the watering system will make your work easier.

Customizing the watering system based on the individual needs of the crop bed ensures there is no overwatering or under watering for each crop bed.

Plastic watering cans are highly recommended. They are cheap, lighter, and require less labor. However, if you want to maintain the beauty of the greenhouse, then you can use metal cans instead.

Another piece of equipment you can use is the trickle watering system. The trickle watering system uses a plastic horse with some outlet nozzles fitted at different intervals on the horse length.

You would place the horse pipes at proximity along the pots. Then, connect the horse to the water storage tank. You should fill the tanks with water consistently. Once full, it will release the water to all the crops.

The horse system will always water the pots and crop bed with a set water quantity and at the same time every day.

Other water equipment you will need in the garden include irrigation tubes, valves, water breakers, sprinklers, a hose, misters, and boilers. Boilers provide excellent temperature regulation.

Energy Conservation Equipment

Due to the high cost of fuel energy, coming up with energy conservation measures will help you reduce the cost of production. Some essential tools for energy conservation include perimeter insulation, energy screens or shades, and windbreakers.

Pest Control Equipment

Every greenhouse structure should have a pest control system. There are different methods you can use to control pests in the farm, some of which use chemicals while others use biological methods.

You can also use natural methods, like beneficial insects, to control pests.

Alternatively, you can use a metal, cloth, or thin plastic mesh to keep pests away from the garden. Fencing and use of door sweeps can also keep the bugs away from accessing specific planting sections.

Depending on which method to use, you can buy sprayers, fogging equipment, and formers.

You can also use insecticide and pesticide to protect vegetables and keep attacking bugs at bay.

CHAPTER 20
Hoop houses & Poly tunnels

Both structures provide a covering for plants that protects them from harsh weather conditions and pests. Both are ideal for extending the growing season.

Before we outline the main differences between them, let's talk about their similarities.

Similarities between a Hoop Houses and a Polytunnel House

Both types of structures are used to extend the growing season. Both options give growers an early start in spring and a longer autumn, such that plants have a longer growing season. This enables you to grow a wide variety of crops.

Both options shield crops from the outside elements such as rain and snow, which gives you control over the moisture levels in the greenhouse. This lessens the chances of destructive diseases and pests. For example, Phytophthora root rot is a common disease that affects plants when excessive rainfall occurs. Both polytunnel and greenhouses protect plants from diseases related to excessive water. They also provide significant protection against animal and insect pests that you may want to keep out of your greenhouse.

Differences between a Hoop Houses and a Polytunnel House

Site Preparation and Construction Details

With polytunnels, there are fewer requirements for site preparation and construction. This makes them an attractive option for beginner greenhouse gardeners. A polytunnel structure can be constructed directly on the ground, even if it is uneven. Furthermore, they don't take too long to set up. The biggest challenge is connecting the polytunnel structure securely to the ground, so that it doesn't blow away in a strong wind.

Greenhouses on the other hand, take a longer time to install, and unlike with polytunnels, they must be placed on a flat and leveled surface that is permanently connected to the structural foundation.

Furthermore, with polytunnels, the ground preparation process doesn't take a lot of time, unlike with a greenhouse, where more precision is needed to prepare the ground for the greenhouse foundation, which is often concrete or gravel.

Purchase Price

Although there are expensive, large polytunnels, these structures are generally cheaper than greenhouses. This is because greenhouses are more highly structured than polytunnels, and often have integrated components like plumbing and electricity. Polytunnels offer lower costs per square foot than greenhouses, yet they still offer high yields.

If you have more money to spend, the cost of a greenhouse with integrated components can be worth it if you really want to maximize your greenhouse experience.

Transportability

When you buy a polytunnel, you have the advantage of knowing that you can move it from one spot to another without a lot of difficulty. This is especially true if you are moving it to a location that is close to the original site. They are very lightweight, so with some help, you can just pick it up and move it.

When you buy or build a greenhouse, you will not be able to easily move it, since they are usually constructed in place in conjunction with a foundation. To dismantle it and move it is even more effort than just building a new one.

Ventilation

Ventilation is crucial because it helps to control humidity, air exchange and temperature. Most plants can dry out or freeze if the temperature changes dramatically. Similarly, an excess of humidity can provide the perfect environment for diseases such as powdery mildew. The ventilation process is different in each type of structure. Polytunnels provide better control over air circulation since they often have large doors on both ends. This provides substantial airflow through the tunnels. Furthermore, you can close them up when you need to.

With greenhouse ventilation, the openings on the roof, door and side vents are crucial to ensure the air gets in. Ventilation is greatly assisted by fans.

Lifespan

Greenhouses can last a lifetime. They are generally sturdy structures with strong coverings on all openings. If you use glass for windows and some of the roofing, you may have to replace panels periodically due to breakage, but overall, the structures don't break down. On the other hand, the covers for polytunnels need to be replaced periodically, and they can be damaged by falling branches, or the structure lifted away by the wind if their anchors are not adequate.

Design

Greenhouses have a myriad of designs available for use, and when put together nicely, it can create a stunning display on a landscape. Design is generally related to the intended end use, the number of integrated components and budget.

Polytunnels don't have many design elements as the structures are standardized. They are often called hoop houses and the design is very practical. They come in many sizes and are covered in plastic. They don't always come with ventilation openings or fixed doorways.

Heat Retention and Shading

Both types of structures protect crops from bad weather and create a suitable planting environment. The plastic sheeting used for polytunnels has less heat retention than a constructed greenhouse. Green polytunnel covers allow less light into the polytunnel, which can reduce the overall temperature and transpiration rate of the plants. This can be advantageous for some crops.

Greenhouses in general provide maximum heat retention while still ensuring adequate light transmission through the glass to the plants. This is because the walls are made of stronger material.

Planting Crops

In greenhouses, plants are generally grown in pots on benches that are raised to waist level, whereas polytunnels are usually used to produce crops directly in the soil or in raised beds. That being said, you can plant in any style using a greenhouse, depending on the type of flooring or foundation you use.

Now you know the differences between a greenhouse and a polytunnel house. This book does not advocate for one particular type of growing structure over another. It is up to you to consider all the information and options and decide what works best for you in your situation at this time.

If you have the money and are planning to stay in the same location for an extended period of time, a greenhouse can offer a longer lasting gardening experience than a polytunnel. A polytunnel has its overall advantages for a beginner gardener. You can get a season or two of growing experience, and then decide if you want to invest in a more permanent structure.

CHAPTER 21
Making a Profit from Your Greenhouse

I f you have a successful greenhouse that grows beautiful plants and flowers, why not consider making some money from your hobby? You might not have ever thought about your hobby as a profitable business, but if you have at least a little bit of extra time and patience, you can actually make quite a nice income from your greenhouse.

Becoming a Business

One of the first things you should do before you actually start conducting business is become a business. This means getting a business name, typically done through your county clerk's office. Most that start a small business use a Doing Business As or Assumed Name; this means that income from your business is the same as income from any other place. You simply add up your income and subtract your expenses and report the final amount on your tax return at the end of the year.

Unless you plan on opening a retail flower store you probably don't need to collect taxes from your customers as you would be considered a wholesaler. However, if your business grows and you're concerned about your need to collect taxes, you can probably quickly speak to a CPA over the phone and ask. Usually applying for a tax ID is very easy and probably done at your county clerk's office as well.

These certificates - your Assumed Name and tax ID - are typically very affordable, usually less than twenty dollars each. Don't hesitate to call your county clerk's office first if you want to be sure your chosen business name isn't already taken or aren't sure which certificate is right for you. You can probably also check online as many counties have their own website where you can run off the forms you need and can find out the charge.

Once you have your business certificates you can open a commercial checking account at just about any bank and may also want to check to see if you can reserve a website name that is at least close to your business name.

Important: When coming up with a business name you can of course have it a bit whimsical; people often assume a greenhouse or flower shop has a bit of whimsy or creativity. Just make sure that it still sounds professional and is easy to remember and spell so that potential customers can remember it and find it again very easily. For instance, you might want to avoid "Debbie's Total Supply of Flowers and Plants from Her Own Greenhouse to Your Table" since it's incredibly long and wordy, but "Deb's Greenhouse and Flower Supply" is much easier to remember!

Finding Customers

So how to find customers and what type of items should you sell? Here are some things you want to consider.

First, make sure your gardening is reliable and that you can grow enough of an inventory on a regular basis so that your customers won't be disappointed. Being able to produce one flowering lily plant is all well and good, but if you want to actually make money from your business you're going to need to produce beautiful flowers on a regular basis.

This will of course mean being very attentive to your greenhouse and your plants. No one wants to buy their flowers from someone who comes through with deliveries only when they can. Yes, you'll lose some flowers here and there and of course can't always count on how many flowers you can actually grow, but to be successful with your business you're going to need to have a pretty reliable idea of what you can and cannot deliver.

Then you'll need to consider what type of customers you can support with your inventory. Flower shops sometimes have their own greenhouse for their supply and supermarkets may have a floral shop but because of how many flowers they need, they may want to deal only with a large commercial greenhouse facility. However there are many other possibilities when it comes to customers that you can support. For example:

- Do you have any mini markets or corner stores near your home that sell a small quantity of flowers? Even if you don't see them selling flowers now, if you were to talk to the manager or owner of the store you might be able to convince them to carry a small inventory.

- Restaurants sometimes want fresh flowers for their tables. You may be able to speak to a manager about providing carnations or other colorful blooms for their dining area or décor.

- Retirement communities also sometimes have fresh flowers on their dining tables; you may be able to provide these for them on a regular basis.

- Businesses often give flowers to their employees on secretary's day or when someone has had a baby or other occasions. If you're priced cheaper than large, national florists you may be able to provide for local businesses when the occasion calls for it.

- Weddings of course are a big business for many florists. While you may not be ready to supply to very large weddings on a moment's notice, if you spread the word among your friends and relatives you might find that someone you know is interested in working with you, especially if your costs are lower than national florists. Many brides today are looking to save money in any way they can so they may be happy to simply choose from the flowers you have available.

- Your friends and family too may want to see what flowers you have available on special days and occasions. They may check with you for anniversaries, birthdays, and holidays.

Very often getting the word out there among your friends and family and local businesses is all that's needed to get your first order, which in turn can lead to so many other orders down the road!

Some Important Considerations

Before you just run out and start talking to those retirements' home managers and restaurant owners, consider some of the following points.

- Consider getting a website even if you don't plan on selling online. A website is actually a great marketing tool because potential customers will often bookmark your site and visit again when they're ready to purchase. A website address is often easier to remember than a phone number, so customers might visit your site looking for your actual contact information. Websites are usually very affordable if you just need a few pages with your contact info and a few photos of your product.

- Most places that purchase flowers from you may expect some type of special packaging. For example, that corner market might be interested in purchasing single blooms that they keep by the cash register for one-at-a-time purchases. However these blooms are usually wrapped in cellophane and may have additional ferns or baby's breath inside. Be prepared with these extra materials and for the wrapping involved; don't just show up with an armful of single blossoms.

- Stores may also expect you to provide the large vase that these flowers are kept in near the register. View this as a marketing opportunity; put a card with your business name and phone number or website address on the front of it.

- Get to know the accessories you need for many of your products. If you're going to provide bridal bouquets, you'll need the little handles they fit into. Boutonnieres for groomsmen usually are attached with a pin. That retirement community may also ask you to provide vases. Shop for wholesale items online so you can purchase these things very cheaply.

- If you're very dedicated about making this greenhouse into a successful business, take a flower arranging class. Putting together bouquets and arrangements is usually part art but part science. Sometimes certain colors or sizes of flowers are just too busy or may look overdone when used together. At the very least, study bouquets you see online and practice some on your own before trying to sell them to a customer.

Another thing you might want to consider about getting customers and selling is to have some marketing material available. At the very least you should have professional business cards made up so that when you call upon potential customers you have something you can leave with them so they have your contact info handy.

You might also be able to make up a flyer or brochure with some featured products. If you can't do this on your own you can easily hire someone with a marketing degree to do this for you; chances are you might even have a friend with some talent that can easily design some business cards or marketing material. Any nearby office supply center can probably print these things out for a very affordable price.

How to set your own prices?

Setting your own price might be a difficult prospect; don't worry most first-time business owners struggle with the question of what to charge their own customers.

There is no right or wrong answer when it comes to the price you should charge others, just some things to consider to come up with your own answer:

- Remember that when you sell flowers to a store for them to sell to their customer, they're going to expect to mark up the price they pay by at least half over again, and usually twice the amount they've paid. This means that if they charge a customer $1.50 for a single bloom, they expect to pay their supplier (that's you) about 75 cents for that bloom. If you think a customer at a store is going to pay $1.50 for that bloom of course you don't charge your customer that much or otherwise they wouldn't make a profit and won't have any reason to sell your item. Consider the price they need to charge and make sure you're being reasonable as their supplier or wholesaler.

- If you don't incur a lot of costs with your own greenhouse you can pass this savings along to your potential customers and gain more business. Larger greenhouses employ a lot of people and have those labor costs as part of their overhead. If you are working alone or it's just you and your spouse, and don't incur a lot of costs for your greenhouse, then you can sell for a much cheaper price than most.

Another thing to consider is just how much of a profit you really want to earn. If you're working with friends and relatives for a wedding or other occasion then of course it's only right that you be compensated for your work but do you need to make as much of a profit as those larger greenhouses and commercial growers? If you're reasonable about your pricing and what you can provide you may get many more customers in the long run.

Remember too that you'll probably make a few mistakes in the first months of your business and may need to raise your prices down the road; don't worry too much about your decision in this regard since many first-time business owners need to make adjustments to these things as they learn more about running their business.

CONCLUSION

Grow your own year-round food in minutes, without the tedious upkeep that goes with ordinary gardening. This basic guide offers a comprehensive how-to for all who choose to grow an 'organic' garden from seed. You'll learn how to use the gardening techniques described in this handbook to cultivate a healthy, bountiful garden with a minimum of effort.

It will also touch on how you can start an operation, as well as present some final tips and tricks that might be helpful for you.

Gardening is a popular pastime for many people, especially those with bigger budgets. However, it takes a lot of time and effort to garden effectively in a greenhouse.

By the time you're finished reading the book, you will be able to grow the most delicious greens and use your greenhouse creatively to grow more than just tomatoes.

Here's what you'll learn:

Why and how to garden effectively in a greenhouse

How to prepare grass clippings for composting and creating mulch

How to create interesting lighting with glass panes to maximize natural light exposure

The best way to keep plants healthy throughout the year with tips from professional landscape designers regarding fertilizing, watering, and aeration of plants within the greenhouse environment.

When you want to grow your vegetable garden or other plants indoors, nothing is more efficient than a greenhouse. A greenhouse is an ideal place for people who live in areas with temperate climates and don't have the proper sunlight to grow their own fresh fruits and vegetables.

Greenhouses can be used to grow a variety of fruits and vegetables indoors, including tomatoes, peppers, cucumbers, beans, eggplants, herbs, and many other types of plants. Growing inside a greenhouse also cuts down on the amount of land needed to grow your own food since you don't have to deal with the elements from outside.

Greenhouse gardening doesn't have to be difficult! Learning how to use the tools and techniques of greenhouse gardening will make you a master at growing all types of plants indoors, from tiny tomatoes to large squash and melons.

We'll show you where different species of plants typically do well in greenhouses and give you methods for planting them accordingly. You'll also learn how greenhouses are constructed and how they can be used for other purposes as well!

The experts at Greenhouse Gardening believe that it's not necessary to be an expert gardener in order to be successful with greenhouse gardening.

Greenhouse Gardening is just one of the many industry certifications Greenhouse Gardening offers its customers.

If you grew up in the northern hemisphere, you probably know of the greenhouse. This is a place where vegetables, flowers, and other plants can grow year after year without ever needing to be outdoors. Greenhouses are a great way to enjoy your gardening hobby in a more controlled environment.

You will also find information on how to use the greenhouse to take advantage of seasonal fruits and vegetables. It is not intended as medical advice or advice for anyone who may have a medical condition or may be pregnant.

Made in the USA
Monee, IL
17 January 2022

89171734R00066